AF809052

Understanding Medicare

Navigating the Confusing Maze of the Medicare System in 2018

NEXT MOUNTAIN
PUBLISHING

Understanding Medicare

Navigating the Confusing Maze of the Medicare System in 2018

This book is typeset in Palatino Linotype 14pt,
somewhat larger than normal, for
easy reading by all audiences.

ISBN: 978-1-7321524-9-6

First Edition. Published July 4, 2018
by Next Mountain Publishing

Understanding Medicare

Navigating the Confusing Maze of the Medicare System in 2018

by Bob Arndt, MBA, EA

and Rick Mortimer

Dedication

This book is dedicated to the 57 million people who depend on the Medicare' system for their health and wellbeing, and in fact often for their very survival.

It's purpose is to guide as many of them as possible towards making the choices that will best serve their continued access to our world-leading healthcare resources as they age to the maximum lifespan each can achieve, without impoverishment at the most vulnerable time of their lives.

Contents

Chapter 1

A Summary of The Medicare Maze

If you are about to turn 65, you are eligible to enroll in Medicare. However, too many people struggle to navigate the complexities of the Medicare program and are overwhelmed by the number of available Medicare insurance plans, the complexities within those plans, and the arduous homework needed to determine their numerous and best choices.

Many Americans believe when they turn 65, they'll be automatically enrolled in Medicare -- which is technically true for anyone already receiving Social Security benefits before turning 65 -- but it is nowhere near that simple. There are still a great many decisions to be made. And not understanding the System and its vast array of options can lead to costly problems, both sooner and later.

If you're not receiving Social Security benefits when you turn 65, you need to sign up for Medicare Part A and Part B either online or at the Social Security office.

If you are eligible for Medicare, you will be receiving an enormous number of offers from Part C and Part D providers. Many of these will be incomplete and self-serving in their descriptions. A very sad fact, unknown to most new Medicare enrollees, is that approximately 75% of all agents licensed to sell Medicare products are only trained and/or certified in one-HALF of the available products. We refer to two "universes" of Medicare add-ons throughout this book, known as Medicare Advantage or Part C, and Medicare Supplements or Medigap policies. You are not allowed to have both, and must pick one or the other. Within each universe, there are a long series of choices and decisions to make, as well.

Seniors face a complicated mix of enrollment periods, different in each universe, which means they need to research their options about how, what, which and when to enroll as they approach their 65th birthday.

This book will help you to make all of those choices. It gets right to the point, guides you to easy to digest explanations and resources that help with your unique situation. It is practical, easy to understand and can save you hundreds or thousands of dollars a year, as well as help you make the best, most timely decisions for your healthcare for the rest of your life.

This book is for individuals who will be enrolling into Medicare or those who want to understand their current Medicare Supplement plan options. It will help you demystify the Medicare maze by simplifying your options on Supplement plan types and costs available to help you determine which is best for you.

Even for us, a former university Professor of Economics, and a former health insurance agent and trust advisor, enrolling in Medicare was a daunting task. The terminology is confusing and the options are numerous, based on the amount of promotional material we received in our mailboxes. The marketing material from insurance companies began arriving six months before the 65th birthday, and after three months, they took up our entire dining room tables. We know nowadays, names and birth dates are for sale to anyone, and insurance companies and agents must be some of the best customers.

Medicare is the single most important aspect of retirement and financial planning for Seniors. This book explains the Medicare System and how to choose what factors to consider. The Medicare rules are complex, but your ultimate results couldn't be more important. Unfortunately, that makes a fairly complete understanding of Medicare a necessity.

Your decisions about Medicare coverage will determine your healthcare for the rest of your life.

Seniors are on their own when it comes to managing and navigating Medicare. The government will offer some guidance as you work your way through the enrollment process, but you must remember that even that advice is not fully impartial. They seem to consistently encourage the choices that the bureaucrats think will keep their costs as low as possible -- which may or may not be the best choice for you.

Sorting through the agendas of the advice-givers can also throw off enrollees who are shifting from employer-based insurance, where a health care plan is created and monitored by the employer's benefits department. To some extent, employer-sponsored health insurance provides a clear path for workers. But in the world of Medicare, seniors must make their own way, from picking their plan to making sure they have enough coverage.

People who are used to employer health insurance can be in for some surprises when they realize they will have to make their own decisions in Medicare, and that it's not an automatic process. The best policy for you won't show up on your doorstep if you do nothing.

Also, you shouldn't design your Medicare coverage for the healthy you, design it for the sick you. It is insurance. You want it to protect yourself from adverse conditions.

Yes, you won't be the first person to try to make sense of it all, only to give up and guess. We strongly encourage you not to do that. The five key factors to consider are:

- What is the status of your financial outlook in retirement?
- Do you have health insurance from another source (like a job)?
- Do you have any chronic conditions or high-likelihood family histories?
- Which doctors and hospitals do you strongly favor using?
- Which prescriptions do you need and where do you want to get them?

This book will also help you to understand why the system is so complex. Medicare has been a work in progress ever since it was introduced in 1965 as a way to provide health insurance for individuals 65 and over or those under 65 with certain conditions – essentially individuals for which health insurance was prohibitively expensive.

In the beginning, there were two parts – A and B.

Part A covered hospital visits and Part B covered outpatient needs.

Since Part A and Part B did not cover 100% of medical costs, this gave rise to an industry of privately run Supplemental (Medigap) Plans to cover costs not paid for by A and B. It is important to know that these uncovered expenses can easily bankrupt a family when a serious illness has to be dealt with. A not-commonly-known fact is that Medicare alone only covers about 50% of the healthcare costs of an average retiree. The other 50% comes from the Your Wallet National Bank, if you don't cover your exposures in advance.

In 1997, Part C plans came in on the tail of the popularization of managed care. Part C plans are also called "Advantage" plans because they are designed to give an "advantage" over just A and B. Advantage plans can cover costs not covered by Medicare such as glasses, gym memberships, hearing aids, etc., while providing a more coordinated care system through a defined network of providers and cost sharing (deductibles, co-pays, "co-insurance") to motivate individuals to stay healthy. The managed care element is a great advantage to the government, too -- it reduces hospital days by 19% and hospital readmissions by 28%, among other notable cost-savings.

In 2006, Part D came into existence when prescription drug costs became a significant part of healthcare delivery. Prior to 2006, some Supplemental Plans provided coverage for prescriptions but after 2006, prescriptions were provided via either stand-alone Part D plans or integrated into Part C plans.

There you go, a quick history of Medicare.

You may be in for a surprise if you're among the many baby boomers we've encountered who believe Medicare is free. It's not. Not only is there an annual deductible, but there are also monthly premiums. Part A is already paid for by past Medicare taxes for most of us, but Part B has a cost, currently $134 per month, deducted from your Social Security check. Part D is usually less than $100 per month additional.

If you don't sign up in your initial enrollment period or when your job-based coverage ends, you will pay a penalty that will raise your premiums for Medicare Part B and Part D for the rest of your life.

Every year you delay signing up for Part B, your monthly premium rises by 10 percent — There is also a waiting period for the coverage to kick in, so you could be without any insurance for several months, perhaps even a year, if you miss the deadline.

For Part D, the penalty is one percent for every month's delay. So a year's delay would add about 12 percent to the monthly drug premium base.

Once you've signed up for Medicare, you should be notified each fall about an open season (officially known as AEP, the Annual Election Period) that allows you to switch plans. This year, that season runs from Oct. 15 until Dec. 7. But AEP allows easy switching only for certain plans (Medicare Advantage), not all of them (Medicare Supplements) — and that may affect what you do when you turn 65.

Open enrollment does not give you a free pass to move from one Medigap plan to another, for instance. Although some plans in some states do guarantee the ability to make a change, Medicare allows most plans to evaluate your health if you try to switch. So if you've developed an illness, you may be rejected or face a sharp rate increase. If you stay with your existing plan, your rates can always rise — but only if they are rising for the plan or group as a whole.

If you didn't pick a benefit package (Plan A, B, C, etc.) you wanted initially, you may not be able to get it in the future.

That's also the situation you could face if you

want to change from a Medicare Advantage plan to traditional Medicare with a Medigap plan.

So what does AEP "open" enrollment really mean? If you're on a Medicare Advantage plan, you can switch to any other plan. You can also switch Part D drug plans annually. And since both Medicare Advantage and the drug plans change premiums, benefits and providers regularly, it's important to review your plans yearly.

Consider more than the cost of the premium when you sign up for a Medicare Advantage or Medigap plan. Look at co-payments and deductibles, too. The cheapest premium might not provide you with the cheapest overall plan. Also, review a company's complaint records as well as its financial stability to hopefully ensure that it will be around as long as you plan to be.

For Medicare Advantage plans and drug plans, the Centers for Medicare & Medicare Services (CMS, the agency that runs Medicare) provides a helpful five-star rating system based, in part, on member satisfaction surveys.

Several companies rate the financial strength of insurance carriers, although you may have to pay to get information. Two of the most frequently cited rating firms are Weiss Ratings and A.M. Best, neither of which charges for basic information.

You may also discover added discounts. If

both you and your spouse decide that a Medigap Supplement is best for you, for example, many companies will give a "household discount" of 5% to 7% to the premiums on both policies, if you both use the one company.

Unless you understand how Medicare is structured, you may not be able to make good decisions about what you're buying. Here is a Summary of Medicare broken down into its different components.

It has three main coverage parts, that together provide a comprehensive medical plan:

- Medicare Part A - This is hospital coverage. It pays for hospital visits, hospice services and nursing home care. Medicare Part A is provided "for Free" to Medicare recipients who have worked and paid taxes for at least 40 quarters (10 years) during their lives.
- Medicare Part B - This is outpatient medical care insurance and includes most services performed outside of the hospital, like doctor appointments, ambulance service. In 2018 the Medicare Part B premium is $134/month for recipients earning less than $85,000-single / $170,000-filing jointly. Citizens who have higher incomes will pay more.
- Medicare Part D - Prescription drugs are covered by this portion of Medicare. Medicare Part

D premiums vary quite widely. In essence Medicare recipients select a "drug" plan from a private insurer and pay a federally subsidized premium for the plan.

While Medicare "covers" nearly all of your medical care needs, it still has deductibles, co-pays, "co-insurance" and other out of pocket costs. And as such, many people choose to purchase a Medicare supplement plan to help limit their financial exposure to these items.

Comparing Medicare supplement plans is a relatively straight forward process as the coverage is standardized. And therefore the only item to compare is the price.

Last but not least, there are Medicare Advantage plans. These policies wrap up all of the elements of Medicare (parts A, B, and D) into one comprehensive package. Here are some highlights:

- Medicare Advantage plans are sold by private insurers.
- When you enroll in one of these policies, it becomes your primary insurance (as opposed to Medicare).
- Private insurers are paid a fixed monthly stipend by the federal government for each Medicare Advantage client they enroll. And in turn, they must follow the Medicare coverage rules.
- Medicare Advantage policies may have

different out of pocket expenses than a traditional Medicare policy. So it's important to have a thorough understanding of the plan before you sign-up.

Medicaid is a comprehensive government health plan for lower income individuals. But many people confuse Medicare and Medicaid. Which is completely understandable considering that:

- They are both government provided healthcare plans
- The names are only a few letters off

But it's important to remember that in general: Medicare is for older Americans (65+) and Medicaid is for lower income citizens.

So, with that broad outline, let's dig in to the details.

Part I

Mapping
The
Maze

Chapter 2

The "Parts" of Original Medicare

Medicare is a single-payer, national social insurance program administered by the US federal government since 1966. It currently works with over 100 private insurance companies across the United States under contracts for administration services. Funded by a payroll tax, participant-paid premiums, and entitlement spending, it provides health insurance for Americans age 65 and older who have worked and paid into the system throughout their working lives. It also provides health insurance to younger people with a major disability status recognized by the Social Security Administration, and people with ALS (Lou Gehrig's disease) or those requiring ongoing renal dialysis.

The program currently provides health insurance to about 57 million people, of which 9 million are younger than 65. As noted, Medicare on average covers only about half the healthcare costs of those enrolled.

BEWARE OF THE TRAP!

Original Medicare covers only about 50% of the average members' total health costs.

This is very important to understand, because most of us have the impression that Medicare is very close to complete coverage. That concept is about 50% wrong.

In today's system, 50% of the costs of anything other than a minor ailment can easily be financially disruptive, even catastrophic.

Here's a related 50% statistic: about 50% of all personal bankruptcies in the US are directly caused by medical bills and collections.

Two more 50% numbers: the median income (2017) for Medicare participants is $26,200, and their median net worth is $74,450. That is not a lot of money to work with, if you are below (indeed, anywhere near) the median.

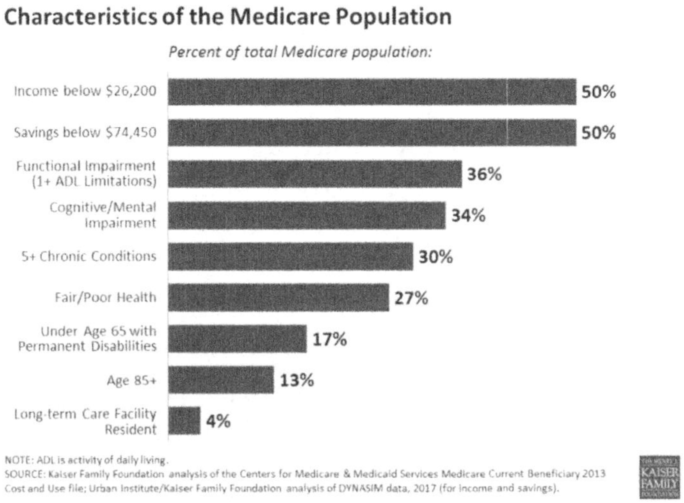

Original Medicare (OM)

Part A

Medicare is broken down in parts signified by letters. **Part A** and **Part B** are considered Original Medicare, and are administered by the Social Security Administration (SSA) and the Center for Medicare and Medicaid Services (**CMS**). *Medicare Part A is for hospital and healthcare facilities coverage.* It includes:

- Inpatient hospital care
- Inpatient care in a Skilled Nursing Facility, after a minimum 3-day hospital stay
- Hospice care
- Home health care

Part A premium payments are "free" for those of us who have worked for at least 40 quarters, or 10 working years throughout our lifetimes. It seems free now, but remember that we have paid in a Medicare Tax of 1.45% of our salaries for many years, matched by another 1.45% from our employer (which could have been paid to us if not for the tax, so it is really We who have paid 2.90% of every dollar we have earned). So it is hardly free in reality.

For those who do not qualify for the no premium version, the maximum amount that you would have to pay for Part A is $413 a month in 2018.

The Part A **deductible**, the amount that you would have to pay the facility before receiving Medicare in a hospital, is $1,340 per benefit period. A benefit period begins the day you're admitted into a hospital or Skilled Nursing Facility, and ends when you've received no inpatient care for 60 consecutive days. The full $1,340 is payable whether you spend 1 day in the hospital, or 100.

If you enter a facility again after the 60 days

has ended, a fresh benefit period will begin, and you will be required to pay $1,340 once again. It is therefore possible to have multiple Part A inpatient deductibles in a calendar year, which would add up very quickly.

Part A **coinsurance** (whenever you see this term, we suggest you convert it immediately in your mind to NONinsurance), the amount that you pay out of pocket after your deductible is met and Medicare benefits have begun, varies based upon the length of time you are an impatient. Coinsurance payments in 2018 are:

- $0 per day, days 1 through 60
- $340 per day, days 61 through 90

If your hospital stay extends longer than 90 days, you will begin using your **60 Lifetime Reserve Days**, and each one will cost you $670 out of pocket. As the term indicates, 60 is all any of us gets, without private add-ons. Beyond that period, your costs will be borne 100% by your wallet.

Part B

Part B is for the services of Doctors and other professional healthcare providers. It covers 2 types of services

- Medically necessary services: Services or supplies that are needed to diagnose or treat your medical condition and that meet accepted standards of medical practice.
- Preventive services: Health care to prevent illness (like the flu) or detect it at an early stage, when treatment is most likely to work best.

You pay nothing for most **preventive services** if you get the services from a health care provider who accepts **assignment**. Assignment means the provider has contracted with CMS , and agreed to accept the **Medicare Approved Amount (MAA)** as full and complete payment for services rendered. Providers do this to simplify their billing practices, and to get paid somewhat quicker. Providers who do not accept assignment are free to bill you for any of their charges exceeding the MAA, but even then are limited to a maximum 15% above MAA, which are known as **Excess Charges**.

For all medically necessary services not considered preventive, you pay coinsurance of **20% of the MAA**, plus any Excess Charges.

Part B covers doctors' charges, nurse practitioner charges, and things like:

- Ambulance services
- Durable medical equipment (DME)
- Mental health
- Inpatient
- Outpatient
- Partial hospitalization
- Getting a second opinion before surgery
- Limited outpatient prescription drugs

Part B does NOT cover:

- Hearing Aids
- Routine Dental
- Vision exams and corrective eyewear
- Dentures
- Cosmetic Surgery
- Accupuncture
- LONG TERM CARE

There are ***no maximums*** to the 20% NONinsurance – you will pay 100% of it Out Of Pocket (**OOP**), without some form of private add-on that caps this amount, with a plan provision known as **MaxOOP**, after which 100% of your expenses are covered.

The 20% can add way up. Taking cancer as an example: 30 radiation treatments will cost over $3,000 each, $90,000 x 20% = $18,000 out of pocket. 6 doses of chemo at $10,000 per dose x 20% = $12,000 out of pocket. Add in physician fees, MRIs, facilities charges, PET scans, exam after exam, etc. etc., and you will easily be on the line for $50,000+.

Or, take heart disease, renal failure, stroke, diabetic crisis, serious infection, or any number of other "treats" life can throw at us.

So, how deep are **your** pockets?

Medicare's publications refer to these sorts of treatments as "covered" — but their definition of covered and ours can vary by hundreds of thousands of dollars!

What Medicare counts as "covered" is based on 3 determinants:

- Federal and state laws.
- National coverage decisions made by Medicare about whether something is covered.
- Local coverage decisions made by companies in each state that process claims for Medicare. These companies decide whether something is medically necessary and should be covered in their area, and are known as **Medicare Administrative Contractors,** or **MACs**.

Now, we move on from "Original" Medicare to the newer parts.

Part C

What is called Medicare Part C is really a plan of administration, rather than a true Part. It is the first of three major types of **private add-ons** that we will encounter. Because SSA and CMS realized that private insurance companies are better at streamlining administrative procedures than government bureaucracies, they supported the creation of private plans called **Medicare Advantage**, synonymous with Part C.

Medicare Advantage (**MA**, or **MA-PD** if drugs are included) is a type of Medicare health plan offered by a private company that contracts with CMS to put systems in place to provide you with, at a minimum, all of your Original Part A and Part B benefits at an equal or lower cost to the government. Most plans offer much more than this minimum, often at a much lower cost.

This is possible because Medicare pays them directly a high percentage of what Medicare would likely spend annually for a person of your age with your specific health challenges. Your Part B premium, the $134 that is taken from your Social

Security check if newly enrolled in 2018, is also paid to the Part C plan sponsor. The better the insurance company does at managing your health, the more of this money they can retain as profit, or to provide extra benefits to their plan members, or both.

The system has numerous checks and counterbalances in it, unlike traditional pre-retirement healthcare plans, to ensure that profit is not the primary driver of of your care. CMS maintains a comprehensive carrier rating system which is geared to patient feedback and quantifiable wellness outcome measurements. Retained profits beyond limited percentages of premiums are penalized. Insurers and providers can receive large bonuses for excellent results; they can also suffer large penalties for poor feedback and outcome metrics. Hospitals with high rates of infections or rapid readmissions can be fined millions of dollars, for example.

In most areas of the country now, it is in fact possible to find excellent MA and MAPD plans with a **$0** monthly premium. The transfer of your Part B premium, $134/mo or so, plus bonuses, is more than enough to maintain profitability for well-managed plans.

Retirees are often stunned that they can pay $0 for a plan that gives them many extra benefits over Original Medicare, like free gym memberships, dental and vision benefits, chiropractic care, hearing aids, etc. But it is true, and now available in a large and growing geographical area. In general, only if you live in a very sparsely populated rural area will you encounter difficulty in finding a low- to no-cost MA or MA-PD plan.

We will take a deeper dive into the benefits and complexities of "Part C" in Chapter 3.

Part D

Prescription drug plans (**PDPs**) make up what is known as **Part D** of Medicare. There are numerous part D plans available, all offered and administered by private insurance companies.

Drug options will vary from plan to plan, and each plan will have its own drug list, or **formulary**. No plan will cover every available drug, especially very new or experimental items (though your doctor may be able to get you into a clinical trial under exceptional circumstances).

At a minimum, all plans must offer at least two drug choices within each broad category of medication. Each PDP establishes a **tiering** system, which drives the out-of-pocket cost model for the participant. Most plans have four tiers, and tier I drugs will always cost less than tier II, etc.

The formulary and tiering for each plan are

available from the plan sponsor before you sign up, and you should check to see how your current prescriptions are listed.

The monthly premium you pay will vary widely depending upon the plan that you choose. Variability is due to formulary differences, deductibles, coverage gap treatment, pharmacy participation contracts, and other items like loss ratios and profit targets.

Note that in addition to standalone PDP's, most Medicare advantage plans now include equivalent prescription drug coverage. This is true even for the MA-PD plans that carry zero dollar monthly premium.

In most cases, you will find that it makes sense to sign up for a PDP or an MA-PD when you are first eligible. Failing to do so, without having equivalent or "creditable" coverage, will result in a penalty which will follow you permanently when you do decide to enroll.

We will cover more details of part D complexities in Chapter 4.

Medicaid

Medicaid is a completely separate social insurance program, not a part of Medicare, although it is also administered at the federal level by CMS, which is actually called the Center for Medicare and Medicaid Services.

It is strictly means-tested and designed to help only the neediest citizens. It is administered by the individual states and funded partially by them, and partially by the federal government. We will discuss Medicaid separately in Chapter 7, and as we break down the programs available to low-income seniors.

Medicare Penalties

Because Medicare is based on the concepts and principles of *insurance,* the system needs participants to enroll as soon as they are eligible, presumably when they are in better health than they will be as they get older. Since the idea of *mandating* that citizens buy insurance was considered unconstitutional taxation prior to Obamacare, the inducement system works instead on a series of **late enrollment penalties** for delaying enrollment.

BEWARE OF THE TRAP!

Missing your earliest enrollment dates in each Part of Medicare can have costly, life-long consequences

The Part A Penalty

If you aren't eligible for premium-free Part A, and you don't buy it when you're first eligible, your monthly premium may go up 10%. You'll have to pay the higher premium for *twice the number of years* you could have had Part A, but didn't sign up.

Example:

If you were eligible for Part A for 2 years but didn't sign up, you'll have to pay the higher premium for 4 years. Usually, you don't have to pay a penalty if you meet certain existing insurance coverage conditions that allow you to sign up for Part A during a special enrollment period.

The Part B penalty

In most cases, if you don't sign up for Part B when you're first eligible, you'll have to pay a late enrollment penalty. You'll have to pay this penalty ***for the rest of your life, as long as you have Part B***. Your monthly premium for Part B may go *up 10% for each full 12-month period that you could have had Part B, but didn't sign up for it*. Also, you may have to wait until the General Enrollment Period (from January 1 to March 31) to enroll in Part B. Coverage will not start until July 1 of that year.

Usually, you don't pay a late enrollment penalty if you meet certain conditions that allow you to sign up for Part B during a Special Enrollment Period, including having had **creditable coverage**, like an equivalent employer-paid plan.

Example:

Your Initial Enrollment Period ended September 30, 2009. You waited to sign up for Part B until the General Enrollment Period in March 2014. Your Part B premium penalty is ***40%***. (While you waited a total of 54 months to sign up, this included only 4 full 12-month periods.) You'll have to pay this penalty *every month*, for as long as you have Part B.

With the Part B premium at $134.00 per month, as it is if starting in 2018, a 40% penalty amounts to $53.60 per month. Over $643 per year, permanently, is a great deal of money: $6,430 if you last 10 years; $12,860 if you make it for 20; over $22,000 if you near the increasingly possible age of 100!

The Part D Penalty

In the full spirit of Medicare, this is another shining example of keeping things as simple as possible. Here we go:

You may owe a late enrollment penalty if, for any continuous period of 63 days or more after your Initial Enrollment Period is over, you go without one of these:

- A Medicare Prescription Drug Plan (Part D)
- A Medicare Advantage Plan (Part C), like an HMO or PPO, with Rx coverage
- Another Medicare health plan that offers Medicare prescription drug coverage
- Creditable prescription drug coverage

The cost of the late enrollment penalty depends on how long you went without Part D or creditable prescription drug coverage.

Medicare calculates the penalty by multiplying 1% of the "national base beneficiary premium" ($35.02 in 2018) times the number of full, uncovered months you didn't have Part D or creditable coverage. The monthly premium is rounded to the nearest $.10 and added to your monthly Part D premium.

The national base beneficiary premium may increase each year, so your penalty amount may also increase each year.

Example:

Mrs. Woolfe is currently eligible for Medicare, and her Initial Enrollment Period ended on May 31, 2014. She doesn't have prescription drug coverage from any other source. She didn't join by May 31, 2014, and instead joined during the Open Enrollment Period that ended December 7, 2016. Her drug coverage was effective January 1, 2017.

For 2017 then:

Since Mrs. Woolfe was without creditable prescription drug coverage from June 2014–December 2016, her penalty in 2017 was 31% (1% for each of the 31 months) of $35.63 (the national base beneficiary premium for 2017) or $11.05. Since the monthly penalty is always rounded to the nearest $0.10, she paid $11.10 each month in addition to her plan's monthly premium, an extra $133.20 for the year.

And for 2018:

In 2018, Medicare recalculates Mrs. Woolfe's penalty using the 2018 base beneficiary premium of $35.02. So, Mrs. Woolfe's new monthly penalty in 2018 is 31% of $35.02 or $10.86 each month. Since the monthly penalty is always rounded to the nearest $0.10, she pays $10.90 each month in addition to her plan's monthly premium., an extra $130.80 for the year.

As we can see, the penalty may change every year, but she will have to pay the calculated amount for the rest of her life (unless she miraculously has no further need of prescription drugs).

Its not really a Penalty, but...

If your modified adjusted gross income as reported on your IRS tax return from 2 years ago is above a certain amount., you'll pay the standard premium amount for Part B and an Income Related Monthly Adjustment Amount (**IRMAA**). IRMAA is an extra charge added to your premium.

Here's the chart:

If your yearly income in 2016 (for what you pay in 2018) was			You pay each month (in 2018)
File individual tax return	**File joint tax return**	**File married & separate tax return**	
$85,000 or less	$170,000 or less	$85,000 or less	$134
above $85,000 up to $107,000	above $170,000 up to $214,000	Not applicable	$187.50
above $107,000 up to $133,500	above $214,000 up to $267,000	Not applicable	$267.90
above $133,500 up to $160,000	above $267,000 up to $320,000	Not applicable	$348.30
above $160,000	above $320,000	above $85,000	$428.60

Chapter 3

Part C is Complicated

• Remember that when Part C is spoken of, **Medicare Advantage** (**MA**) is the topic.

Medicare Advantage plans are the fastest growing source of comprehensive coverage for people on Medicare.

Enrollment in private Medicare Advantage health plans has increased in recent years, and 30 percent of Medicare beneficiaries were enrolled in Medicare Advantage plans in 2014 (up from one-fourth in 2010). Medicare beneficiaries who enroll in private Medicare Advantage plans often receive supplemental benefits that are not covered under traditional Medicare, such as vision and dental benefits. Medicare Advantage plans are required to have an annual limit on beneficiaries' out-of-pocket expenses, or **MaxOOP**, for Medicare Part A and Part B covered services of $6,700 in 2014. After that amount, the plan pays 100% of covered items. In Medicare Advantage, the coinsurance (NONinsurance) element is still present, but it is at least limited.

A Kaiser Family Foundation analysis, featuring the latest publicly available data on the 2017 Medicare marketplace, examines new information on plan availability, premiums, out-of-pocket limits and other features of Medicare Advantage plans. Overall, the analysis finds that the Medicare Advantage market has been relatively stable in recent years, with few changes in premiums, plan offerings, and insurer participation. Key findings include:

- The average Medicare beneficiary will be able to choose from 19 plans in 2017, a number which has been relatively stable since 2012.
- While premiums have been relatively flat, average limits on out-of-pocket costs for Part A and B benefits have increased by 25 percent since 2011, from $4,281 in 2011 to $5,332 in 2017.
- About one-quarter of beneficiaries will have a choice of plans offered by three or fewer firms in 2017.

The two most widely available plan types are Health Maintenance Organizations (**HMOs**) and Preferred Provider Organizations (**PPOs**). Together, they served 18.1 million of the 19 million MA and MA-PD plan members in 2017, **95.3%** of the total. Several other types of plans (PFFS, Cost Plans, MSAs, Pilot Programs, Programs for All-inclusive Care for the Elderly (PACE) etc.) are offered in 4.7% of situations, but that is a whole 'nother set of jargon that almost no one needs to remember — so let's skip it (refer to Medicare.gov if you are in the 4.7%, and be prepared to slog through many pages).

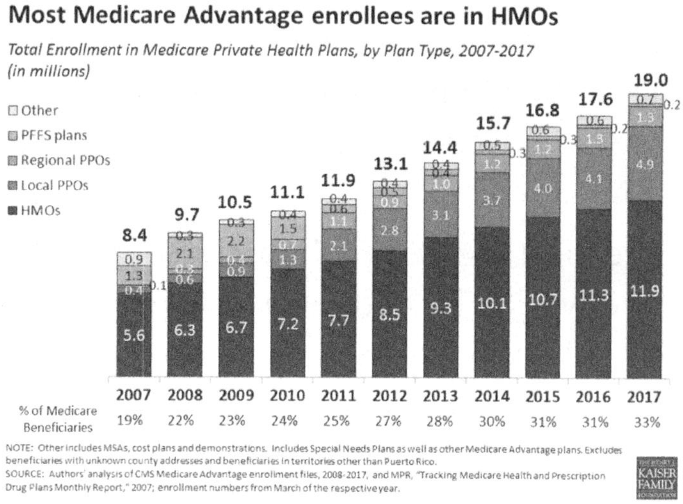

The primary difference between the two main types is that HMOs coordinate **all** of your care through your chosen Primary Care Provider (**PCP**), who may be an MD or a DO in family practice or internal medicine, and must be a member of the plan's network.

He or she is responsible for ensuring that all of your other care providers are acting in your best interest, are properly credentialed, and are also contracted within your plan's network. Many plans pay significant "wellness" bonuses to doctors with the best patient improvement records, and for things like extremely thorough annual checkups. He or she will get to know all aspects of your health better than any specialists who might be needed, and will be responsible for making any such referrals. In an HMO, a comprehensive selection of specialists is maintained in-network, and your care providers will need to be on this list for your plan to cover your care.

The most significant limitation of an HMO is that its network will tend to be local to your home counties. If you travel extensively, or if you maintain seasonal residences in different areas, it will not be your best choice.

In a PPO, by contrast, you also have a PCP and a local network (and sometimes a state-wide network), but you are **not required** to use providers solely within that network, nor are you required to get a referral to see a specialist. If you venture out-of-network, though, you will pay substantially higher co-pays and NONinsurance, and your maximum annual out-of-pocket exposure will be higher.

The ability to get care in other areas of the country without having to carry that load entirely out of your own wallet makes a PPO the clear winner for folks who travel a fair amount, or those with seasonal homes. Or for anyone who objects to being strictly confined to one specific network of providers. As a general rule PPOs are more expensive plans than HMOs, measured by monthly premiums, co-pays. and MaxOOP. But they are not nearly as expensive as Medigap supplements, while providing the same ability to choose *any* provider.

BEWARE OF THE TRAP!

Do not choose an HMO
if you might travel, or have
a secondary residence

If you're enrolled in a Medicare Advantage Plan, most Medicare services are paid for directly by the insurer. and aren't paid by SSA as under Original Medicare, All MA plans are *required* to cover everything that Original Medicare does, and most in fact cover much more. The only difference you will immediately notice is that you will present your MA plan card to service providers rather than your original red, white and blue Medicare card.

Most Medicare Advantage plans also offer prescription drug coverage, and pretty much the only reason you wouldn't want the MA-PD flavor is if you have better prescription drug coverage from your employer, the VA, or TRICARE.

Very importantly, Medicare and CMS have been strongly advocating these types of plans because they introduce some cost savings by utilizing managed care models. CMS encouragement comes in the form of bonuses for meeting preventative care goals and customer ratings, and can result in very large year-end payouts to insurers. Also, because insurers are compensated more for patients with more treatment-intensive conditions, profitability tends to be more predictable and less dependent on the specific risks of a plan's pool of members, as is the case in Medigap policies (the other universe of plans, coming up in Chapter 5).

A huge resulting benefit of these encouragements to insurers is that many have found it profitable to offer MA and even MA-PD plans at *zero monthly premium cost to enrollees*, while offering substantially more benefits that Original Medicare.

By contrast, Medigap plans, or Supplements (next up), do not provide any cost savings from managed care approaches. This can be better for the participant, but considerably more expensive for Medicare, since a retiree is free to choose the best, most well-known, most expensive hospitals in the country for dread disease care, if desired. Many high-end institutions [Mayo Clinic, Cleveland Clinic, Johns Hopkins, MD Anderson, etc.] do not accept Medicare as full payment, and even with the best Medigap coverage, the patient may have to pay large sums, often up-front. This is one of many reasons that Medigap premiums tend to rise faster each year than those of Medicare Advantage.

Medicare Advantage Special Needs Plans (**SN**Ps) are types of HMOs designed for members with specialized needs. They must always include Prescription Drug Coverage.

Dual SNPs (**D-SNPs**) are offered to members who qualify and are enrolled in both Medicare and Medicaid, based on financial need, and we will discuss these and other programs in Chapter 7 on Medicaid.

C-SNPs are special needs plans for folks with chronic diseases, and are specially designed to accommodate the extra services and therapies associated with these conditions, including:

- Chronic alcohol and other drug dependence
- Autoimmune disorders
- Cancer (excluding pre-cancer conditions)
- Cardiovascular disorders
- Chronic heart failure
- Dementia
- Diabetes mellitus
- End-stage liver disease
- End-Stage Renal Disease (**ESRD**) requiring any mode of dialysis
- Severe hematologic disorders
- HIV/AIDS
- Chronic lung disorders
- Chronic and disabling mental health conditions
- Neurologic disorders
- Stroke

I-SNPs are for people who are living in an institution, either in a nursing homes or confined at their own home with nursing assistance.

One special characteristic of all **SNPs** is that ***they have open enrollment year-round.*** You may leave one plan and re-enter one that is better for you, at anytime, with 1 month's notice.

Zero Premium Plans

According to the Kaiser Family Foundation, one of the best independent watchdogs of the Medicare program, in 2017, as in prior years, most Medicare beneficiaries (81%) had a choice of at least one "zero premium" MA-PD, which charge no monthly premium for coverage of Medicare Part A, B, **and D** benefits , other than the standard monthly Part B premium collected before you get your Social Security check, which is then turned over to the MA plan insurer. Plans can offer zero-premium MA-PDs partially by using their rebate (the difference between the plan bid and the maximum federal payment or benchmark) to reduce the equivalent Part D premium.

While seniors have said that premiums are an important factor in their plan choice, the data indicate that other factors must also play an important role. Among MA-PD enrollees with access to a zero premium plan (97% of all MA-PD enrollees), only about half (52%) are enrolled in such a plan.

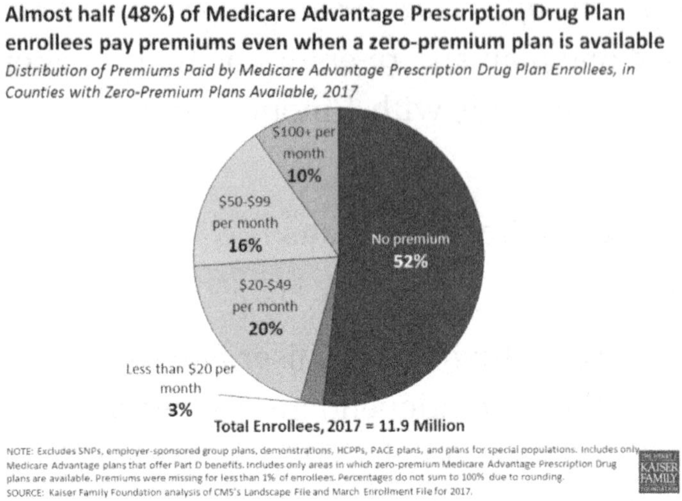

More than one-quarter (26%) of MA-PD enrollees with access to a zero premium plan are in plans with premiums of $50 per month or more, including 10 percent with premiums of $100 per month or more.

Two reasons for this appear likely: 1) the participants are unaware that they personally qualify for a zero-premium plan, since marketing education by agents to participants is severely limited, or, 2) their plans have slowly increased premiums, knowing that seniors have a strong avoidance of change to a new system, and are likely to remain if the monthly charge is affordable.

If diving into data about MA and MA-PD plans interests you, as it does us, here is some deeper information from the Kaiser Family Foundation's Medicare Advantage Spotlight for 2017. If it just glazes your eyes over, feel free to skip ahead to Chapter 4 without fear of missing any crucial points :-)

Market Concentration. UnitedHealthcare and Humana together account for 41 percent of enrollment in 2017; enrollment continues to be highly concentrated among a handful of firms, both nationally and in local markets. In 17 states, one company has more than half of all Medicare Advantage enrollment – an indicator that these markets may not be very competitive.

In most states, three firms or affiliates account for more than three-quarters of Medicare Advantage enrollment

Combined Market Share of the Three Firms or Affiliates with the Largest Number of Medicare Advantage Enrollees by State, 2017

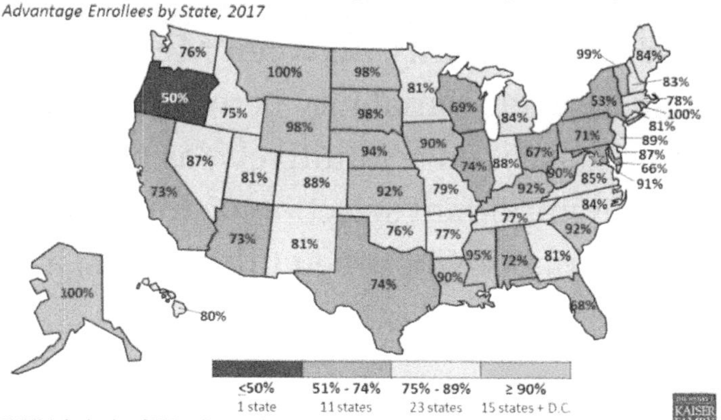

SOURCE: Authors' analysis of CMS State/County Market Penetration Files, 2017.

Medicare Advantage Penetration. At least 40 percent of Medicare beneficiaries are enrolled in Medicare private plans in six states: CA, FL, HI, MN, OR, and PA. In contrast, fewer than 20 percent of Medicare beneficiaries are enrolled in Medicare Advantage plans in 13 states, plus the District of Columbia.

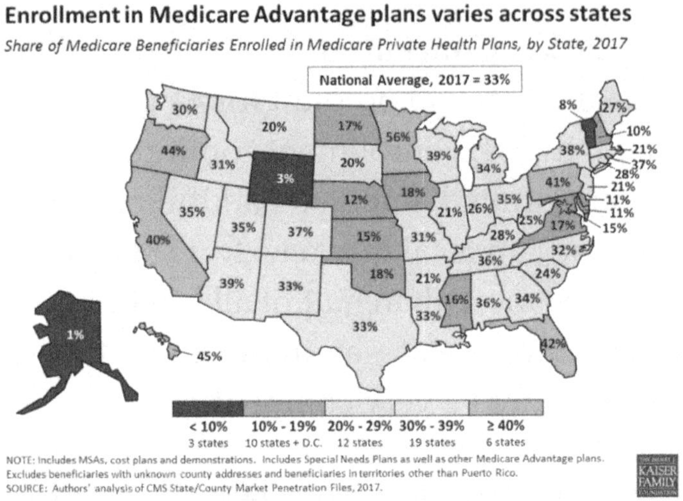

Wide Variability Between Metros: MA market penetration variability between urban and rural areas makes sense intuitively, as network density is an important selection factor. But there is surprising variability between urban areas, as well.

Figure 5

Medicare Advantage penetration varies widely across large metropolitan counties in 2017

Five Counties with the Lowest and Five Counties with the Highest Penetration Rate, among Counties with at least 100,000 Beneficiaries

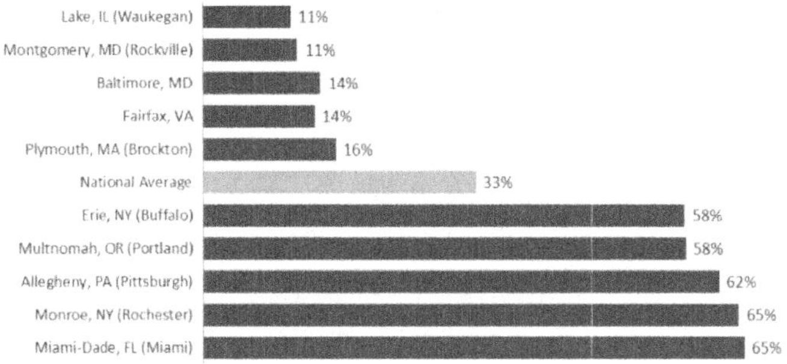

NOTE: Excludes beneficiaries with unknown county addresses or in territories other than Puerto Rico. 109 counties had at least 100,000 beneficiaries in 2017. Estimates for Baltimore County (13%) and Baltimore City (17%) were averaged. Counties' seats are denoted in parentheses when different from county name.
SOURCE: Authors' analysis of CMS's March Enrollment files for 2017.

Premiums and Cost-Sharing. While average Medicare Advantage premiums paid by MA-PD enrollees have been relatively stable for the past several years ($36 per month in 2017), enrollees may be liable for more of Medicare's costs, with average out-of-pocket limits increasing 21 percent and average Part D drug deductibles increasing more than 9-fold since 2011; however, there was little change in out-of-pocket limits and Part D drug deductibles from 2016 to 2017.

Weighted average monthly premiums for Medicare Advantage Prescription Drug plan enrollees vary across the country

Ten States with the Lowest and Ten States with the Highest Average Monthly Premiums, 2017

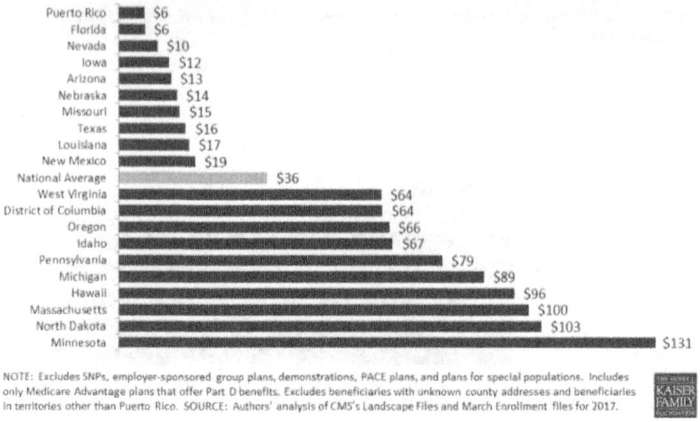

NOTE: Excludes SNPs, employer-sponsored group plans, demonstrations, PACE plans, and plans for special populations. Includes only Medicare Advantage plans that offer Part D benefits. Excludes beneficiaries with unknown county addresses and beneficiaries in territories other than Puerto Rico. SOURCE: Authors' analysis of CMS's Landscape Files and March Enrollment files for 2017.

Out-of-pocket limits for Medicare Advantage Prescription Drug plan enrollees have increased between 2011 and 2017

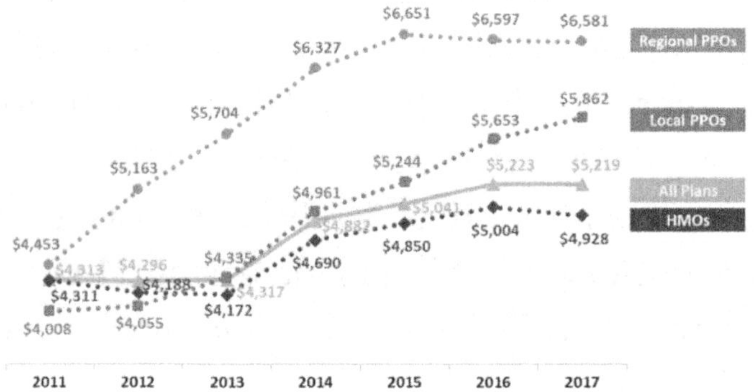

NOTE: Excludes special needs plans (SNPs) and employer group health plans. Percentages may not sum to 100% due to rounding. In 2017, plans with 4% of enrollees were missing information about out-of-pocket limits. Includes only Medicare Advantage plans that offer Part D benefits. SOURCE: Authors' analysis of CMS Medicare Advantage enrollment and landscape files, 2011-2017.

Medicare Advantage enrollment is projected to continue to grow over the next decade, rising to 41 percent of all Medicare beneficiaries by 2027 (from less than 25% in 2010).

It is very clear that large forces, both

governmental and market-based, are working to expand the role of MA plans in Medicare. As private plans take on an even larger presence in the Medicare program, it will be important to understand the implications for beneficiaries covered under Medicare Advantage plans and traditional Medicare, as well as for the alternative universe of private add-ons, the Medigap supplement products.

Both will continue to have a place in serving retirees, and more education will be required to help those turning 65 to discriminate between the two, and make rational choices.

Medicare Advantage and MA-PD Deadlines

BEWARE OF THE TRAP!

Do not miss any of these deadlines that apply to your situation

☠ ☠ ☠ ☠ ☠ ☠ ☠

The end of the third month after the month of your 65th birthday. Your Initial Enrollment Period (**IEP**)for Parts A and B, as well as Medicare Advantage, lasts seven months, centered on the month in which you turn 65.

Month 1	Month 2	Month 3	65	Month 5	Month 6	Month 7

One year after you start a Medicare Advantage or MA-PD plan, if you want to change to Original Medicare plus a Medigap supplement and a standalone Prescription Drug Plan (PDP), after trying Medicare Advantage.

During this time, you have a **Guaranteed Issue Right** (no medical questions of any kind, so no medical underwriting) to get into a Medigap plan, if you did not like the MA plan you had. This is called your **MA trial right**.

December 7th of each year. This is the end of the Annual Enrollment Period (**AEP**), during which you may add, remove or change Medicare Advantage or Part D Drug Plans. AEP runs from October 15th through December 7th.

February 14th of each year. This is the end of the annual Medicare Advantage **Disenrollment** Period (**MADP**), which runs for January 1st to February 14th. During this time, you can drop a MA or MA-PD plan and return to Original Medicare, but you may **not** change to another MA plan. Just to keep things easy, right?

February 28th of each year. This is the end of the annual Part B General Enrollment period, which runs from January 1st. During this time, you can enroll in Part B if you missed your IEP opportunity.

Note that it is necessary to have both Part A and Part B in effect before you are eligible to sign up for Medicare Advantage (Part C). Soooo— if you missed you IEP chance to do all three at once, you will need to act during 1/1 to 2/28 to get Part B, and then *act again* between 10/15 and 12/7 to get MA or MA-PD! Of course, all seniors are supposed to intuitively know this, because MA agents are not allowed to contact them directly to inform them of it. But that's OK because, as we know, Medicare is so *simple.*

Chapter 4

Part D is for Drugs

Medicare Part D plans offer coverage for prescription drugs, administered through private insurance companies. There are numerous stand-alone Part D plans available, and many more that are embodied within Medicare Advantage Prescription Drug (MA-PD) plans. Drug options will vary from plan to plan, and each plan will have its own drug list or **formulary**. All plans must cover every therapeutic category of prescription drug, with at least two choices within each category.

PDPs place drugs into different **tiers**, or copayment levels, within their formularies. A drug in the lower tier will generally cost less than a drug in a higher tier, and your copay will be less.

All part D plans must have a process in place

for members to request exceptions to the drug formulary. This is usually achieved by having your physician or pharmacist initiate the process with the plan, by requesting an exception. It is also often possible to request a tiering-level exception if the expected copay will produce a financial hardship for a participant.

The monthly premium you pay will vary based on the company and the plan you choose, and premiums vary widely, as do formularies and tiering levels.

Having a well-qualified agent working with you will enable you to know in advance the tiers and costs of the drugs prescribed for you. Be aware that tiering may change within a plan year, and specific drugs can also be dropped or added within the year. When this happens, if it adversely affects you, Medicare will normally enforce a 30 to 60 day window, within which the plan must continue giving you the drugs you have become used to. During this time, you can initiate an appeal of the policy change.

Prescription drug plans are reasonably attentive to customer requests for exceptions, because CMS grades each plan continually, using a 1 to 5 star rating system. An important part of a plan's rating is patient satisfaction. If a plan falls to a 2 star rating, it will receive very negative attention from CMS and Medicare, including the possible suspension of the plan's ability to enroll new members. This gets the immediate attention of senior management, as you can imagine!

See the comments in the glossary about using the word "grievance" should you need to escalate a request for an exception.

Be aware that if you go without Medicare part D prescription drug coverage, or other coverage through an employer or retiree plan that is at least as comprehensive as part D coverage, for 63 consecutive days or more, you will be charged a late enrollment penalty once you initiate part D coverage. See the section on penalties, at the end of Chapter 2.

BEWARE OF THE TRAP!

Avoid falling into the Donut Hole, if you can

Medicare drug plans have a **coverage gap** (also called the "Donut Hole"). This means there's a temporary limit on what the drug plan will cover for drugs.

Not everyone will enter the coverage gap. The coverage gap begins after you and your drug plan have spent a certain amount for covered drugs. In 2018, once you and your plan have spent $3,750 on covered drugs, you're in the coverage gap.

One of the most difficult things to understand in Medicare coverage is how deductibles and co-pays work within PDPs. Amounts change somewhat each year, but for 2018, they break down as follows:

The first $405 of your prescription drug cost in a plan year is paid 100% by you, as a **deductible**.

You then enter the **Initial Coverage Period (ICP)**, during which your co-pay per drug will be determined by your plans formulary and tiering system, with the balance paid by the plan. These co-pays are fixed, realtively small, and clearly disclosed in the promotional material for the plan. Your OOP cost cannot exceed 25% of the total cost of the drug, and much less in some plans, with Tier I and Tier II generics.

Once you and your drug plan, combined, have spent $3,750, you hit the **Initial Coverage**

Limit, and enter the dreaded **Donut Hole**.

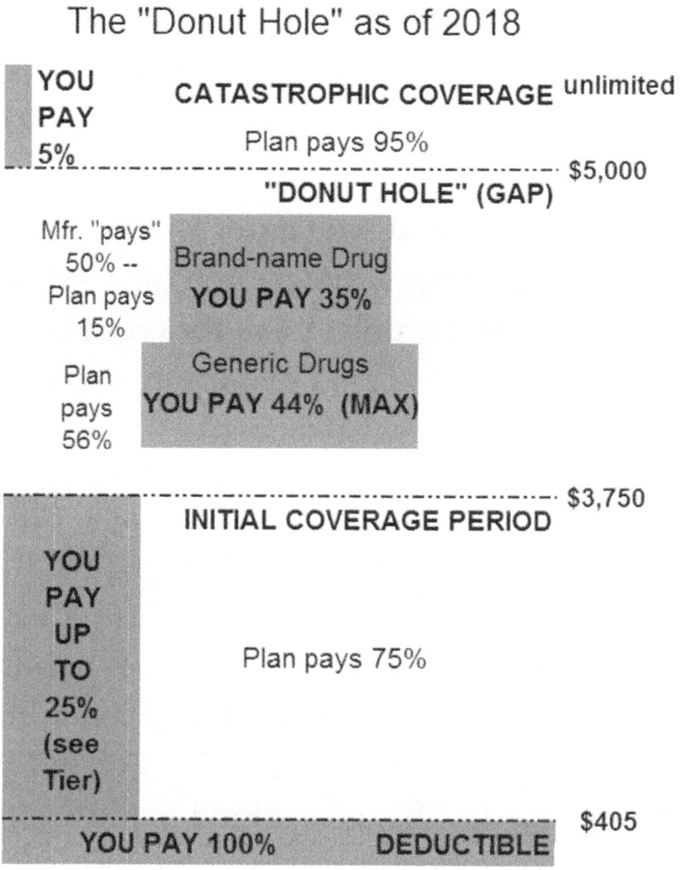

During the Donut Hole, or Coverage Gap, in 2018 you will pay 44% of the price of generic drugs, and your plan will pay 56%. For branded drugs, you will receive a 50% discount from the manufacturer, and a 15% contribution from your plan, but you will be required to pay the remaining 35% out-of-pocket. This continues until your total **True Out-of-Pocket Costs** (**TrOOP**) hit the coverage gap limit of $5,000. Note that the 50% discount that the manufacturer "pays" towards your Brand-name drugs **actually counts** towards your TrOOP, which can accelerate your exit from the coverage gap quite a bit. So TrOOP isn't all *truly* out of pocket cost, is it?

Beyond this limit, you enter what is known as **Catastrophic Coverage**, and for the remainder of the year you will pay only 5% of the cost per prescription, with 15% paid by your plan and the remaining 80% paid by Medicare.

Brand-name Drug Example:

In 2018, Mrs. Anderson reaches the coverage gap in her Medicare drug plan. She goes to her pharmacy to fill a prescription for a covered brand-name drug. The price for the drug is $60, and there's a $2 dispensing fee that gets added to the cost. Mrs. Anderson pays 35% of the plan's cost for the drug and dispensing fee ($62 x .35 = $21.70).

The amount Mrs. Anderson pays ($21.70) plus the manufacturer discount payment ($30.00) count as out-of-pocket spending. So, $51.70 counts as out-of-pocket spending and helps Mrs. Anderson get out of the coverage gap. The remaining $10.30, which is 15% of the drug cost and 65% of the dispensing fee paid by the drug plan, doesn't count toward Mrs. Anderson's out-of-pocket spending.

If you have a Medicare drug plan that already includes coverage in the gap, you may get a discount after your plan's coverage has been applied to the drug's price. The discount for brand-name drugs will apply to the remaining amount that you owe.

Generic Drug Example

In 2018, Mr. Evans reaches the coverage gap in his Medicare drug plan. He goes to his pharmacy to fill a prescription for a covered generic drug. The price for the drug is $20, and there's a $2 dispensing fee that gets added to the cost. Mr. Evans will pay 44% of the plan's cost for the drug and dispensing fee ($22 x .44 = $9.68). The $9.68 he pays will be counted as out-of-pocket spending to help him get out of the coverage gap.

If you have a Medicare drug plan that already includes coverage in the gap, you may get a discount after your plan's coverage has been applied to the drug's price.

Items that count towards the coverage gap:

- Your yearly deductible, coinsurance, and co-payments
- The discount you get on brand-name drugs in the coverage gap

- What you pay in the coverage gap

Items that don't count forthe coverage gap

- The drug plan premium
- Pharmacy dispensing fee
- What you pay for drugs that aren't covered

If you think you've reached the coverage gap and you don't get a discount when you pay for your brand-name prescription, review your next "Explanation of Benefits" (**EOB**), which your plan should be mailing to you at least quarterly. If the discount doesn't appear on the EOB, contact your drug plan to make sure that your prescription records are correct and up-to-date. If your drug plan doesn't agree that you're owed a discount, you can file an appeal.

Here is some *great* news about the Donut Hole: unless Congress changes the rules in the next two years, it will disappear in 2020. This will represent a large cost-saving for participants, as well as a significant easing of the complications of calculating your out-of-pocket exposure.

By 2020, you'll pay no more than 25% for covered brand-name and generic drugs during the gap—the same percentage you pay from the time you meet the deductible (if your plan has one) until you reach the out-of-pocket spending limit (up to $5,000 in 2018), after which you get the Catastrophic Coverage co-pay of only 5%.

Year	You'll pay this percentage for brand-name drugs in the coverage gap	You'll pay this percentage for generic drugs in the coverage gap
2018	35%	44%
2019	30%	37%
2020	25%	25%

This change will be helpful and very welcome to those with high drug expenses.

BEWARE OF THE TRAP!

If your drug cost are sure to be very high, you must budget for very high co-pays at some point in the year. Try to get through the Hole quickly by using Brand Name drugs

If your prescription drug costs are predictably high, failing to budget for the Donut Hole can cause great problems. Remember that each year, the calculations restart. First, the deductible hits in January. If you need a LOT of expensive drugs, you could possibly be into the Donut Hole as early as March, and have to lay out another $1,250, per person, very quickly. So be certain to budget for this expense rather than trying to forego needed meds; save an extra $100 or so per month throughout the year, so you can "blast through" the Donut Hole quickly, and get to the 5% co-pays on the other side!

Also, pay attention to the fact that Brand Name drugs get a 50% manufacturer discount during the Hole, and this **counts** towards your supposed "true out of pocket" spending amount, even though it does not come from your pocket! The more of the $1,250 gap amount that can be covered by these discounts, the less you will have to come up with in cash. And the **faster** you may be able to exit the Hole and get to the nice 5% co-pays on the other side. If the calculations prove advantageous to you, talk to your doctor about switching to a Brand Name drug for a month or two to save cash money.

Here is some more good Donut news: most PDP plans now have some coverage within the gap, as do most drug plans embedded within Medicare

Advantage (MAPD) plans. Often, Tier I and Tier II generics continue to have the same low co-pay as normal.

Some less-good news though: as new high-cost specialty drugs have become available, Medicare Part D spending in the catastrophic coverage ("reinsurance") phase of the benefit has increased as a share of total drug benefit costs, from 14% in 2006 to 38% in 2016.

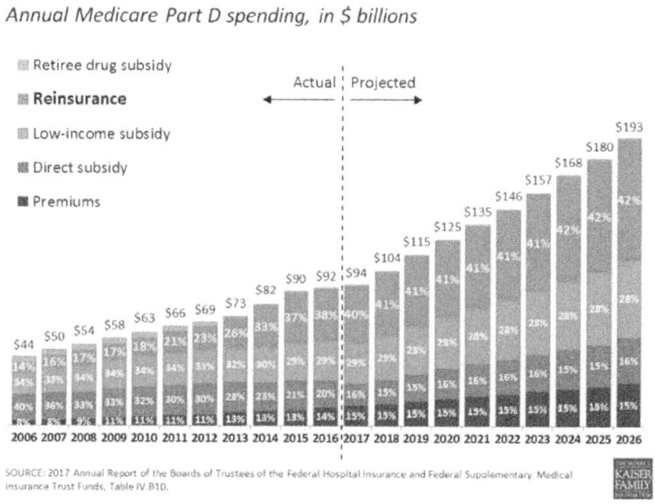

This implies that, at some point, our esteemed congress will feel the need to step in with another "fix", and we can expect it to require more out of our pockets. Enjoy it while you can.

Note that the details of what happens with **Low Income Subsidy (LIS)** prescription drug qualifying participants are too much more complex to address here. Generally speaking, the higher the percentage of LIS a person qualifies for, the lower will be the OOP cost, even within the Donut Hole. For those with full dual eligibility for both Medicare and Medicaid, the Donut Hole disappears completely. Those of our readers who want all of the intricate calculations, the most comprehensive explanation we have found is here:

https://q1medicare.com/PartD-The-2018-Medicare-Part-D-Outlook.php

Chapter 5

The "Plans"

Medicare Supplements,
a/k/a "Medigap" Insurance

Medigap policies, also called **Medicare Supplement Insurance**, are sold by private insurance companies and help cover Medicare's cost-sharing requirements, and fill gaps in the benefit package.

Medigap policies assist beneficiaries with their coinsurance, co-payments, and deductibles for Medicare-covered services. They help to shield beneficiaries from sudden, out-of-pocket costs resulting from an unpredictable medical event. They also allow beneficiaries to more accurately budget their health care expenses, and reduce the paperwork burden associated with medical claims. In most cases, patients just go to their provider and receive care, paying nothing out of pocket depending on coverage plan selected, and the provider does the work of collecting from the insurer. In 2017, just over one in five Medicare beneficiaries had an individually-purchased Medicare supplement insurance policy.

Currently, there are 10 standardized Medigap plans (labeled Plan A through N; Plans E, H, I, and J are no longer available for sale. Plans C and F will stop enrolling new members on 1/1/2020, leaving just 8 choices). All Medigap policies of the same letter-type provide the same benefits. Premiums vary by plan type, insurer, age of the enrollee, state of residence, sex, and **non-tobacco status**. Outside of your Initial Enrollment Period, medical underwriting will probably be required, and you may easily be declined coverage.

Medigap plans are **standardized** by federal law, meaning that a Plan A from one company in Colorado will pay for exactly what a Plan A from another insurer in Pennsylvania will pay for. There is no difference to you as the policyholder. There may be slight differences in how quickly each company pays your doctors and providers, but there is no material difference for you.

The distinctions are between plan letter-type, as to what is covered. The most important other difference to you is the **price** you pay each month, and factors influencing how that price might increase over time. Once you have selected a plan type and company, if your health declines, you may be stuck with that company as long as you need to retain the coverage. Companies are free to raise prices annually, as long as they do so for entire age groups, and not for individual medical reasons.

How many retirees use Medigap policies vs. Medicare Advantage? Here's a graph, again from KFF's fabulous data mine, that shows how the trends changed from 2000 to 2010:

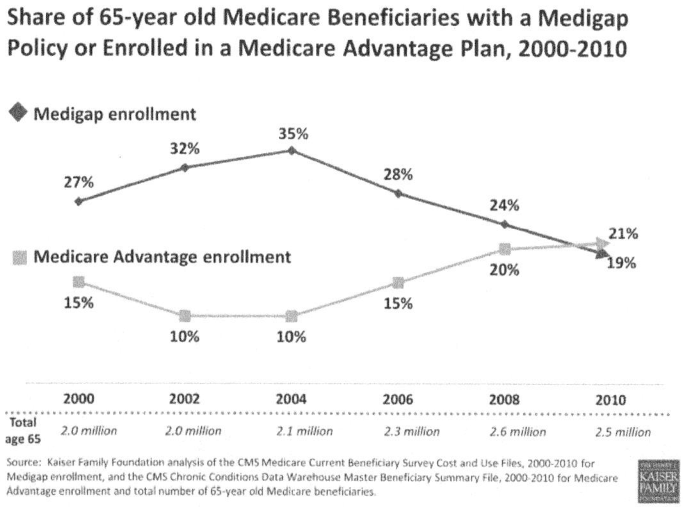

The decline in Medigap enrollment leveled out after this snapshot, and it now has about a 23% share of the retiree market. Medicare Advantage continued to climb, and is now about 30%. This is in large part due to overt efforts of federal administrators to reduce the overall costs of Medicare, and a primary tool has been the reduction in "first dollar" insurance coverage. They want us to have to pay, at least something, for everything, to reduce usage. Here are the Plans:

GAPS IN MEDICARE BENEFITS % covered per Plan Year	A	B	C New enrollmt ends on 1/1/2020
Part A coinsurance and hospital costs up to 365 days, after Medicare benefits are used up. Without Medigap, these amounts are **$335 per day** for days 61-90, plus **$670 per day** for days 91-150, then **100%** out of your pocket.	100%	100%	100%
Part B coinsurance or "NONinsurance", which is **20%** of Medicare covered services	100%	100%	100%
Blood (first 3 pints) **$130 to $450** per pint	100%	100%	100%
Part A hospice care coinsurance or copayment, typically **5%**	100%	100%	100%
Skilled nursing facility care coinsurance - after 3+ day hospital stay, $0 fo days 1-20, **$167.50** days 21-100, then **100%** out of your pocket. NOTE even with Medigap, there is **no coverage** without the hospital stay. Requires separate Long Term Care insurance policy or MEDICAID SPEND-DOWN to get coverage.	no	no	100%
Part A deductible -- **$1,340** per initial hospital stay, 60 day reset	no	100%	100%
Part B deductible, **$183** per year	no	no	100%
Part B excess charges, **100%** of amount exceeding Medicare approved charge by up to 15%	no	no	no
Foreign travel exchange (up to plan limits)	no	no	80%
Out-of-pocket limit** or MaxOOP, except foreign travel	N/A	N/A	N/A
Out-of-hospital Prescription Drugs -- SEPARATE PART D PRESCRIPTION DRUG PLAN IS NECESSARY	no	no	no

Medigap Plans 2018

D	F*	G	K	L	M	N
	New enrollmt ends on 1/1/2020					
100%	100%	100%	100%	100%	100%	100%
100%	100%	100%	50%	75%	100%	100%***
100%	100%	100%	50%	75%	100%	100%
100%	100%	100%	50%	75%	100%	100%
100%	100%	100%	50%	75%	100%	100%
100%	100%	100%	50%	75%	50%	100%
no	100%	no	no	no	no	no
no	100%	100%	no	no	no	no
80%	80%	80%	no	no	80%	80%
N/A	N/A	N/A	$5,240	$2,620	N/A	N/A
no	no	no	no	no	no	no

* Plan F also offers a high-deductible plan. If you choose this option, this means you must pay for Medicare-covered costs up to the deductible amount of $2,240 in 2018 before your Medigap plan pays anything.

** After you meet your out-of-pocket yearly limit and your yearly Part B deductible, currently $183 per year, Medigap Plan G pays 100% of covered services for the rest of the calendar year.

*** Plan N pays 100% of the Part B coinsurance after your annual $183 deductible, except for a copayment of up to $20 for some office visits and up to a $50 copayment for emergency room visits that don't result in inpatient admission.

The desire to eliminate first dollar coverage is why, for example, Medigap Plans C and F have been phased out — they cover even the Part B deductible, currently only $183 per year, which otherwise has to come from your wallet on the first doctor visit of the year. The geniuses at Office of Management and Budget are convinced that this one change will save $400 million per year overall. We doubt it, but C and F are gone as of 2020 anyway.

Medigap has its own set of rules, and in most jurisdictions, has a different set of education and licensing requirements for insurance agents, compared to Medicare Advantage.

BEWARE OF THE TRAP!

Working with Half-an-Agent

☠ ☠ ☠ ☠ ☠ ☠ ☠

A surprisingly large number of insurance agents are only licensed to sell Medigap policies within the Medicare space, because the additional licensing requirements to be able to sell Medicare Advantage policies are quite grueling. There is an additional education course required (with a fee), sponsored by the organization of America's Health Insurance Plans (**AHIP**), including a stringent initial testing requirement ***and*** the need to re-test annually (with more fees, of course). In addition, ***each carrier*** of Medicare Advantage plans has its own specific coursework and tests, again required to be completed ***every year,*** and many carriers require that agents who will sell in more than one state —

or even in more that one ***region*** within each state – complete a ***separate*** certificiation for ***each region, each year!*** This is a very burdensome set of time and cost hurdles, especially for agents who want to represent several carriers in order to offer their clients the best possible fit in every set of circumstances. It can easily add up to over a month of lost productive time, unpaid, just completing certs and testing. That is a lot to ask. Its like an extended unpaid vacation – without the vacation!

Seen from the inside, it is less surprising that so many agents convince themselves that Medigap plans are enough to suit all possible needs, ***but they are not***.

When all one has is a hammer, everything begins to look like a nail.

As retiree's health and finances differ, and as they change over time, both major types of coverage must be considered, with all of their many intricacies. The key question to ask any insurance agent that you are considering working with is:

"What carriers are you appointed with for Medicare Advantage, and what carriers are you appointed with for Medicare Supplements?"

His or her answer will be factually verifiable with your state insurance commissioner, and ***it needs to contain at least several carriers within***

each of the two categories. At the least, you will know that your agent has taken the great time (and expense) to learn as much as he or she can about Medicare and the specific products available in your area, before going out to hunt for commissions.

If you do not get the right answer here, we strongly recommend politely ending the interaction at the first opportunity. Any information that you receive from an incompletely licensed agent is at best suspect, and at worst, dangerously misleading. Why deal with a person who is not totally serious about providing clients the best professional advice possible, without worrying about whether the best product choice for you is something that can help him sustain a living for his family? It is hard to be impartial when one choice puts food on the agent's family's table, and a better choice for the client does not.

Asking this one question will also communicate very clearly to the agent that you have much more education on the subject that the average prospective client, and that he or she will have to be working at their highest level, and prepared to be held to the highest ethical standards. The words *appointed with* are very precise in the insurance industry, and convey a higher level of knowledge about the rules of the game.

Perhaps we shouldn't find this surprising, yet we do: there are also a huge number of books and websites which focus only on Medicare Advantage coverage **OR** Medigap supplement coverage, but treat the other approach ***as if it did not exist at all***. We consider this to be a disgraceful practice, because it leaves intelligent consumers, who are diligently trying to do their homework in an already complicated area, with the impression that they have explored all their options. It is far worse to think you know the whole story and act accordingly (possibly with devastating long-term consequences), than it is to realize that you still do not have all required information, and keep seeking. Do not stop until you have explored ***all*** of the options, to find the one best suited to your individual needs.

BEWARE OF THE TRAP!

Doing your research
using books or websites
that only tell you
half of the facts

Particularly with websites, we see that information presented as impartial, complete editorial content often is just a clever mask for steering consumers to companies and agents who will pay the publisher for referrals or sales. And it is exceedingly difficult, even for the most knowledgeable researcher, to confidently distinguish impartial advice from hopelessly slanted commercial manipulation.

With books and websites, you as a consumer do not get to ask a direct and pointed question to ensure that the information you are about to receive comes from a fully informed and impartial source. The best you can do is to make sure that both "universes" of products are covered with equal completeness and emphasis. Look for these terms throughout the material:

Medicare Advantage Universe	**Medigap/MedSupp Universe**
Part C	Supplements
MA or MA-PD	Plan A, B, C, D, F, G, K, L, M, N

Within Medigap supplements, the primary differentiator is price, the amount you pay in monthly premium. We've heard agents compare buying a Medigap plan to buying a TV; if you are buying the same model, would you rather pay $800 at a department store, or $400 at a Walmart? Easy choice.

BEWARE OF THE TRAP!

Buying ONLY on price, paying too little for Medigap coverage

However, there are more subtle differentiators with Medigap policies that even many agents do not notice, but which can cost you big bucks and health opportunities if you miss them. A major one is the ability to switch between plan types as your needs change, without medical underwriting. Only a few companies offer this, and the rules are different even between initial plan types within the same insurer. If you miss this, or if it is not offered in your jurisdiction, your first decision of plan type will be the one you are stuck with, should your future health picture include any of a number of ailments that will result either in a refusal to issue a new policy, or a greatly increased premium.

Medigap policies, once issued, are **guaranteed renewable** year after year, although *the premiums will increase as you age*. But unlike health plans within Obamacare, for example, you will not be able to switch carriers at will, without consequence for **preexisting conditions**, even though you have maintained continuous similar coverage. Outside of your **initial election period**, or a few specific circumstances which create a **special election period**, the ailments you have acquired, the drugs prescribed for you, and even your height vs. weight, can easily result in a decline to issue from another carrier.

Because renewability is guaranteed, but premium amount is not, another set of important differences between carriers goes to their ratings, their loss ratios, and their pricing history within age brackets. Highly rated companies tend to be more conservative across all of their business practices, and thus more stable and predictable with premium increases.

Yet another important element is how each plan computes its rates. There are three possible methods: Attained Age, Issue Age, and Community Rated. **Attained Age** policies will increase the premium every year as you age, since costs get higher with age. This is like a pay-as-you-go pricing scheme. The idea is that you only pay for the age you've attained; these policies tend to be cheaper in the beginning, with the largest annual rate increases of the three types, especially far in the future.

Issue Age policies are *theoretically* priced one time, based on age at enrollment. The premium when issued is usually higher than Attained Age, to account for the increasing costs over time by taking in more money during the early years. But these plans can still increase rates as costs increase or as Medicare's rules change, as long as the increase is not tied specifically to age. There is no such thing as a "fixed price" Medigap plan. Issue age plans have become less popular because people who do not understand the distinction see only a higher price, and tend to buy the cheaper rate. In general, these plans comprise less than 10% of all offered plans, and are not even available in many locales.

Community Rated plans are also less than 10% of offerings. These plans have uniform pricing in large areas, perhaps a state or a large portion of a state. The rates are the same for a given enrollment age regardless of zip code, and *regardless of sex*. So women, who normally pay less than men, pay the same. Not such a good deal for the girls, but the rates do tend to be more stable over the years than Issue Age. The rate difference can cancel out for a couple, and with the addition of a **household discount** (available on most plans of all 3 types, when both domestic partners sign up with one company), can be the cheapest overall choice.

For all types of plans, a company experiencing unusually high **loss ratios** (the percentage of collected premiums actually paid out to health providers for claims) is likely to soon experience unusually high rate increases as well. Your agent should be able to provide you with as much of this data as you care to wade through. And he or she should be able to distill it all down to an overall recommendation as to carrier.

BEWARE OF THE TRAP!

Paying too much for Medigap coverage

There are always large price differences between carriers, even within specific plan types within the same geographical region. All else being equal (which is of course impossible with the number of factors influencing pricing), the lower priced policy within the same plan category (A, C, F, N, etc.) will be the better value. As long as your agent has done the work necessary to have numerous choices in his or her bag to offer you, you have the best chance of being able to trust his or her advice on which to pick.

BEWARE OF THE TRAP!

Missing your moment
can cost you your ability
to obtain Medigap coverage
forever

☠ ☠ ☠ ☠ ☠ ☠ ☠

The single most important variable in buying any Medigap plan is in fact ***when*** you choose to buy it. Unlike Medicare Advantage plans, Medigap policies are **medically underwritten** if you buy your coverage outside of very limited time periods.

This means answering tough health questions, conforming to height/weight tables, and not taking any of a long list of disqualifying drugs. Insurers are only able to control the risks of their overall pool of members by greatly restricting **bad** risks outside of guaranteed issue periods — and they do so zealously,

And of course, to keep things as *simple* as possible, the limited time period definitions are completely different for Medigap plans versus Medicare Advantage plans!

For Medigap, the best time to buy is *within the six month period beginning on the day you first sign up for Medicare Part B*, the original doctors' services portion of Medicare. ***Missing this window by even a day can mean losing the option of having Medigap coverage permanently***, if your health is less than optimal.

If you start receiving Social Security benefits at age 62, or anytime before your 65th birthday, *you will be automatically enrolled in Part B on the* ***first day*** *of the month in which you turn 65*. Six months from that day is one day too late.

If you waited to elect Social Security income until your 65th birthday or later, *you must proactively contact SSA and request to be enrolled in Part B*. Starting Part B begins your six-month countdown window to get Medigap coverage without medical questions of any kind.

What does Medigap coverage cost?

The only honest answer is "it depends", but that is not very helpful. So we've distilled down some market statistics to get you into the ballpark. These prices are all based on the preferred risk category that is assigned to non-smokers who enter a plan in their initial six-month window. Rates can easily be double those shown for an obese, unhealthy, smoking male. We will look at geographic area and plan type only, to keep the comparison as simple as possible.

The states in the lowest decile of average Medicare Supplement costs **across all plan types** include:

- New Mexico
- Oklahoma
- Utah
- Wyoming
- New Hampshire

The five states in the highest decile for average supplement cost include:

- New York
- Nevada
- Illinois

- Indiana
- Wisconsin

In 2015, the national average for all monthly premiums was **$184**, according to Gorman Health Group's report of December 1st, 2016.

For Medigap **Plan F**, currently the most popular plan type in the country with an overall 55% market share, the following are the average monthly premiums by state, for those with the highest and lowest in 2015:

Highest:

- New York $217
- Massachusetts $218
- New Jersey $215
- Florida $205

Lowest:

- North Carolina $170
- Virginia $168
- Pennsylvania $168
- New Mexico $164

These figures, also from Gorman, are deceptively smooth, though. A live search of rates in Westchester County, NY, for a male, 65, non-tobacco, Plan F shows rates ranging from **$292 to $482**. In Bernalillo County, NM (Albuquerque), the range is **$130 to $318**. You can see that that is almost a **four-times** spread from highest to lowest, for the same benefits for the same human! These figures come from data aggregator CSG Actuarial, a major source of live quotes for agents nationwide, and they are accurate as of March 2018.

Further, the New Mexico quotes include two from a single insurer, one at **$134.32**/mo. and the other at **$317.50**/mo. What is the difference? We could be wrong, but it appears to be purely a matter of **agent choice**; does he or she want to deliver the lowest cost to the client, or is it more important to earn a **136% higher** commission?

That is a lot of difference for the agent. Other than cost, the plans will perform identically for the client. With Medigap policies, there can be huge variation in price and agent compensation. This is **not true** of Medicare Advantage policies, where commissions are standardized by Medicare and enforced by CMS.

BEWARE OF THE TRAP!

Choosing an unscrupulous or incompletely informed agent

Know your agent! All else equal, a skilled high-producing agent will know that keeping the client in the long run is the key to success in the senior markets, and will not be concerned with pocketing a few hundred more dollars. He or she will also know that the business written at ripoff prices will not stick on the books, because another agent **will** find, and be happy to take away the client at a fair price.

So **which plan should you pick**? *It depends!* There are so many variables that determine price, and then the variations that we've shown above even at the price level. But we are not going to duck the question many of our readers want answered. Instead, we will take an example, and go through some of the reasoning that you should do, applying your own criteria.

Google says that Lebanon, Kansas is the exact geographical center of the USA. So we will start there, Zip code 66952. We're looking at rates for a 65 year old male, non-smoker, during his Initial Enrollment Period, so no medical underwriting of any kind will be required. To further simplify, we will look at the rates of only one company (which we won't identify, but which consistently places in the lowest quintile of rates that we've quoted). Survey says:

Plan	Price/month
A	$116.99
F	$146.24
HDF	$43.04
G	$116.33
N	$100.29

OK, a few things jump out at you here. First, where are Plans B, C, D, K, L, and M? They are not available from this carrier – and that is very common. Most insurance companies only go to the trouble of quoting the plan types that are most in demand. So out of the 10 (+1) theoretically available plan types, only 5 are real contenders. The (+1) is

HDF, meaning High-Deductible Plan F, which means that You get to pay the first $2,240 of costs in 2018 and every year thereafter, before the plan kicks in anything. If you are extremely healthy and have great genes and healthy parents who lived to be 100, this is a good low-cost option. Or if $2,240 per year is an acceptable permanent risk for you.

Let's analyze the numbers for the other choices. The only difference between Plan F and Plan G is that G does not cover the Medicare Part B deductible, currently $183.00 per year. This number will go up from year to year, but so will our premium – so it is valid to analyze it at this moment in time. The monthly difference in the premiums is $29.92, or $358.92 per year.

Would you rather pay an extra $183.00 per year, or an extra $358.92, spread out over 12 months? Hmmm. We'll take the $183. The G over the F is the best choice in this case, saving something like $1,759 over 10 years, even if you use the maximum benefit every year.

Another thing about Plan F: because it is the most popular plan now, and it ends new enrollments in 2020, we know two things: first, the pool of members will age over time, since new 65 -year -olds are not able to join. An older pool means higher costs, so premiums will tend to rise faster than non-terminated plans. Second, since the insurers know that plan members will not be able to replace an existing Plan F with a new Plan F without the dreaded Medical Underwriting, they will not fear raising premiums as much as usual, putting a double whammy on premium increase probabilities over the coming years.

This Plan A seems way overpriced for the least coverage, including exposure to as many as four $1,340 hospital deductibles in a really bad year. So, no.

High Deductible F saves over $1,200 per year in premium, but exposes you to $2,240 in each year before the plan pays anything. How strongly do you want to bet on your continued great health?

So G looks good, but is N better? The only difference is whether your doctor **accepts assignment** from Medicare, since doctors who do are prohibited from hitting you with excess charges. Even if they do not, the maximum additional they can charge is 15% of the MAA, so your exposure is low.

If you are willing to ask every doctor you go to "do you accept Assignment from Medicare?", and find someone else if the answer is no, then N is your plan.

Price Increases as You Age

We know that a Medigap policy will experience rate increases virtually every year, as the participants age. Insurers are allowed to increase rates at will (subject to state regulatory approval, rarely withheld), as long as the rate increases apply to entire classes of policyholders.

So, how afraid of that should you be?

We would advise that you should have the means to pay premium increases of 3% to 10% in any given year, without having to seriously consider giving up your plan.

Over an extended time, the increases may add up to a doubling of your premium. Remember that one of the best reasons for choosing Medigap over Medicare Advantage is that your extra outlays are predictable, and that this is especially important if you are in ill health.

It would be a shame to pay in every month for 15 or 20 years of good health, only to have to revert to higher deductibles, co-pays and coinsurance when your medical bills really start piling up!

The only thing predictable about premium increases is that they will happen. Choosing more solid insurers and lesser exposed plans should help to keep them limited, but nobody can predict the rate of change with any certainty.

With that said, let's go back to our Lebanon, Missouri example and look at how the rates increase with applicant age:

Plan	Male 65 NS Price/month	M 75 NS	M 85 NS	M 95 NS	M 99 NS
A	$116.99	$147.51	$182.39	$226.72	$226.72
F	$146.24	$184.39	$239.98	$298.32	$298.32
HDF	$43.04	$54.27	$70.63	$87.79	$87.79
G	$116.33	$148.41	$187.90	$236.34	$236.34
N	$100.29	$125.36	$165.70	$210.98	$210.98

Plan	Female 65 NS Price/month	F 75 NS	F 85 NS	F 95 NS	F 99 NS
A	$103.26	$130.20	$160.98	$200.11	$200.11
F	$129.07	$162.75	$211.81	$263.30	$263.30
HDF	$37.98	$47.90	$62.33	$77.49	$77.49
G	$102.67	$130.99	$165.85	$208.60	$208.60
N	$88.51	$110.64	$146.14	$186.21	$186.21

Overall, these increases look bearable, unless your budget is already stretched when you start Medigap. You will need to take a hard look for yourself, though.

If the potential increases look scary to you now, it might be best to choose Medicare Advantage before you invest large monthly dollars in a plan that you are likely to let lapse.

Medigap Deadlines

By far, the most important deadline in the Medigap universe is the last day of the six-month period following when: 1) you turn 65; **and,** 2) you have initiated Medicare Part B coverage. The starting date of this period will usually be the first day of the month in which you turn 65, if you are receiving Social Security benefits. Otherwise, you will need to have directly contacted your local Social Security office to start your Part B benefits, and with them, your monthly premium payments ($134 in 2018).

If delayed, without equivalent creditable medical insurance coverage (employer-sponsored), you will be hit with Part B penalties for life.

65	Month 2	Month 3	Month 4	Month 5	Month 6

Missing this deadline means losing your **only certain opportunity** to enroll in a Medigap supplement policy, at the lowest rates, without any medical questions or underwriting of any kind. Insurers **must** issue to anyone and everyone during this IEP for Medigap.

BEWARE OF THE TRAP!

Missing this deadline!

☠ ☠ ☠ ☠ ☠ ☠ ☠

Other than this hard calendar point, you may have a salvation in one of the following **Guaranteed Issue Rights** (also called "Medigap protections"), which are the rights you have in certain situations (a/k/a Special Election Periods) when insurance companies must offer you certain Medigap policies without medical underwriting. In these situations, an insurance company:

- Must sell you a Medigap policy
- Must cover all your pre-existing health conditions
- Can't charge you more for a Medigap policy because of past or present health problems

In most cases, you have a guaranteed issue right when you have other health coverage that changes in some way, like when you lose the other health care coverage.

In other cases, you have a "**trial right**" to try a Medicare Advantage Plan (Part C) and still buy a Medigap policy if you change your mind. You have a guaranteed issue right (so an insurance company can't refuse to sell you a Medigap policy) in these situations:

- You're in a Medicare Advantage Plan, and your plan is leaving Medicare or stops giving care in your area, or you move out of the plan's service area.
- You have Original Medicare and an employer group health plan (including retiree or COBRA coverage) or union coverage that pays after Medicare pays and that plan is ending.
- You have Original Medicare and a Medicare SELECT policy. You move out of the Medicare SELECT policy's service area.
- You joined a Medicare Advantage Plan or Programs of All-inclusive Care for the Elderly (PACE) when you were first eligible for Medicare Part A at 65, and **within the first year of joining**, you decide you want to switch to Original Medicare. (Trial Right)
- You dropped a Medigap policy to join a Medicare Advantage Plan (or to switch to a

Medicare SELECT policy) for the first time, you've been in the plan **less than a year**, and you want to switch back. (Trial Right)

- Your Medigap insurance company goes bankrupt and you lose your coverage, or your Medigap policy coverage otherwise ends through no fault of your own.
- You leave a Medicare Advantage Plan or drop a Medigap policy because the company hasn't followed the rules, or it misled you.

Note: There may be times when more than one of the situations above applies to you. When this happens, you can choose the guaranteed issue right that gives you the best choice.

Can you buy a Medigap policy if you lose your health care coverage? Possibly. You may have a guaranteed issue right to buy a Medigap policy. Make sure you keep these items, and contact your local Social Security Administration office:

- A copy of any letters, notices, emails, and/or claim denials that have your name on them as proof of your coverage being terminated
- The postmarked envelope these papers come in as proof of when it was mailed

You may need to send a copy of some or all of these papers with your Medigap application to prove you have a guaranteed issue right.

If you have a Medicare Advantage Plan but you're planning to return to Original Medicare, you can apply for a Medigap policy before your coverage ends. The Medigap insurer can sell it to you as long as you're leaving the plan. Ask that the new policy take effect no later than when your Medicare Advantage enrollment ends, so you'll have continuous coverage.

BEWARE OF THE TRAP!

Missing the deadlines on any of these "backup plans" for getting Medigap

Chapter 6

MediGap vs. Medicare Advantage

Now that you have a good understanding of the two "universes" of private Medicare add-ons, let's dig in to the practical differences between them. By the end of this chapter, you should find yourself naturally favoring one or the other.

After a discussion of Medicaid in the next chapter, we will be ready to lay out a strategic framework for solidifying your decision with confidence, and for knowing when and how you might consider shifting tactics — as you age, as your health changes, as your financial situation changes, and as changes in the Medicare framework and available products roll out over time.

Digesting all the material in the last few chapters was a tough climb up the side of a mountain! It starts to level off here, and you will find it much easier to follow along.

The best way to start a decision analysis between two major choices is often to list out the

Pros and Cons of each, then examine those consequences. We encourage you to do that from your personal point of view, knowing what you now know. We will start two lists for you, and encourage you to add or scratch items as you see fit.

PRO MEDIGAP SUPPLEMENTS	CON
Absolute Choice of Health Providers	Can Only Get Without Underwriting for 6 Months Following 65th Birthday + Part B
Absolute Predictability of Expense (with Ancilary Products)	High Ongoing Monthly Premium Cost, Whether You Use Services or Not
Choice of Plan Types/Coverage	Definite, but Unknown, Future Premium Increases
Plans are Standardized by Law	Need for Multiple Ancillary Products
Most Plans Inherently Limit Annual OOP costs	Must Buy Separate Prescription Drug Coverage
Some International Travel Coverage Available	Lack of Dental
Rsk of Major Additional Expense can be Eliminated (excepting Nursing Home LTC)	Lack of Vision
Net Net, Much Cheaper with Bad Health, if Enrolled Without Medical Underwriting	Lack of Hearing
Available in Some States for Disabled, ESRD, ALS under 65	Lack of Podiatry
	Lack of Chiropractic
	Lack of NURSING HOME LTC
	Complexity
	Significant State by State Variation in Eligibility, Guaranteed Issuance, Premium Controls, etc.

PRO	MEDICARE ADVANTAGE / MA-PD CON
No Medical Underwiting or Upcharge for Bad Health (except ESRD)	Limited to chosen Network Providers -- Must Follow Rules to be Fully Covered
Low to Zero Premium Cost	Dates You Can Enroll or Switch Limited by Law
Premium Cost Trending Even Lower	Must Get Referral to See Specialist (except PPOs)
Simplicity	Co-pays, etc., Trending Higher
No Pre-Existing Condition Limitations	Little Domestic Travel Coverage
Favored by Medicare/CMS	No International Travel Coverage
Largest Share of Retirees	Unpredictable NONinsurance
Usually Include Prescription Drug Plan	Unpredictable Deductibles, Co-pays
Always Have Annual MaxOOP -- but set HIGH	Risk of Major Additional Expense
Can Switch Into Annually, without any Medical Underwriting	Limited Differences in Coverages Available -- between Insurers
Net Net, Cheaper with CONTINUING Good Health	Can Negatively Impact Existing Employer Retirement Plans (State, VA, Tricare etc.)
	Lack of Major Dental
	Lack of NURSING HOME LTC
	Need for Ancillary Products

Note that both lists seem to have more Cons than Pros. But the simple number of entries is misleading, because small specifics are spelled out. ***In virtually all cases, You WILL be better served by choosing one or the other, versus staying with only Original Medicare.*** OM simply leaves your exposure far too high.

We suggest you go through the lists with two colored markers, highlighting things that are good and positive for you with one, and things that are negative for you with the other. This small exercise will go a long way towards clarifying your thinking.

In the broadest sense, the more you favor maximizing your healthcare options and provider choices, the more you will tend to like Medigap.

The more you favor minimizing your ongoing, constant expense, whether you need care or not, the more you will tend to like Medicare Advantage.

In Chapter 8, we will expand on these broad generalities to give you a framework for a more comprehensive decision.

Before we leave this chapter, it is important to mention some variability in Medigap rules that do not apply to Medicare Advantage.

These affect primarily the issue of being able to get Medigap coverage at the lowest price without the denial risk of medical underwriting, when you are *outside* of the 6-month Initial Election Period following 1) turning 65, and 2) signing up for Medicare Part B.

Nationwide, if you joined a Medicare Advantage plan for the first time and you decide to leave it within 12 months of joining, you may have a guaranteed issue right to buy a Medigap plan:

You may be able to return to your same Medigap policy that you had before you joined an

Advantage plan if the insurance company still offers it. If it is no longer available, you will have a right to buy another Medigap policy.

Whether or not you received prescription drug coverage from your Medigap policy before you switched to Advantage, your new Supplement policy can't have drug coverage (which would only apply if you had a policy issued before 2006). However, you may be able to sign up for a Part D plan.

You can apply for any Medigap policy at any time you are not already committed to a Medicare Advantage plan (such as during the Annual Election Period, October 15th through December 7th each year, if you have MA), but you will be subject to medical underwriting, higher rates, and a 6-month exclusion for pre-existing conditions.

Also, state laws in **New York** and **Connecticut** require most Medicare Supplement plans to be available year-round **without** price adjustments for health status. This is equivalent to a never-ending Medigap Special Enrollment Period.

If you live in **California**, **Maine**, **Missouri**, or **Oregon**, and you already have a Medigap Supplement plan, then you may qualify for a Medigap Special Enrollment Period.

At certain times during the year, these four states allow you to transfer to any Medicare

Supplement plan that has equal or lesser benefits than your current policy.

The actual Special Enrollment date depends on either 1) your birthday, or 2) when you enrolled in your current plan. Check with your preferred insurance carrier or your state insurance commissioner's website for more specific information, if you live in one of these states.

Finally, special rules apply in 30 states for Medicare recipients under age 65, who are there because of total disability, ESRD or ALS. We have provided a table of these rules in our Reference section.

Chapter 7

Medicaid and Long Term Nursing Care

These are two topics that do not seem to belong together. One is about a poverty-level social safety net, the other is about lengthy stays in a nursing home late in life. Yet we will see that they are closely related for a great many older seniors.

Before we look at that connection, we need to look at what has happened to the established alternative, Long Term Care (**LTC**) insurance.

LTC policies issued long ago typically paid only for nursing home care, with confusing decisions required, such as how much of a daily/monthly benefit to buy, and whether specific nursing home coverage was likely to be enough to cover all probable exposure. Today, most policies are comprehensive and cover a wide range of services in a variety of settings, including nursing homes, assisted living communities, adult day care centers, Alzheimer's special care centers and your own home. As coverage has expanded, and costs of care have multiplied, prices have increased even further.

This is unfortunate, as LTC policies from even 20 years ago were prohibitively expensive for most families. Still, if you are well-off and can qualify, this is worth investigating.

One current alternative to plan for long-term care expenses is through a policy that combines life insurance with long-term care insurance. The popularity of these policies has taken off in recent years, with over 100,000 sold annually. These policies provide long-term care benefits and pay out a death benefit to life insurance beneficiaries if not all of the long-term care coverage is used.

But these forms of coverage are still out of reach for many families. Leaving us with...

Medicaid

Medicaid is completely separate from Medicare, a social insurance program strictly means-tested and designed to help only the neediest citizens of all ages, not just those over 65.

It is administered by the individual states and funded partially by them, and partially by the federal government.

This is the main federal-state program that provides health and long-term care coverage to low-income people, and is a source of supplemental coverage for nearly 10 million Medicare beneficiaries with low incomes and modest assets. These beneficiaries are known as **dual-eligible beneficiaries** because they are eligible for both Medicare and Medicaid.

Qualifying as a Dual Eligible

A person who is enrolled in both Medicare and Medicaid can only be there by virtue of very low income and assets. The limits for 2018, in general, are **$1,032/month** in income if single, with $2,000 in available assets. Married couples face even tougher qualifying, with a combined income limit of **$1,391/month** and $3,000 in assets.

Be sure to check with your local office of the state department of social services or its equivalent to see if you can qualify, if you think you are even close to these limits. A caring case worker may be able to find ways to qualify you if he or she is convinced that you have undue hardships without help. And nobody can know the intricacies of the purposely obscure qualification process better than an insider.

It is absolutely worth the effort to gain these benefits. **Dual Eligibles** are able to get special zero premium Medicare Advantage plans known as Dual Special Needs Plans (**D-SNPs**) that have deductibles, co-pays and coinsurance reduced to near-zero as well. They also include subsidized prescription drug coverage.

This is the closest thing to a C**ongressional health plan** that you can get, without being elected to congress! All care that that is medically necessary will be made available, virtually without limit, and at little or no cost to you. And contrary to what you may think, there is little to no stigma attached to being a Medicaid recipient and a member of a D-SNP.

Prescription drugs cost $0.00 or $1.20 (Tiers I and II), and no more that $3.70 for the most expensive new brand names. Dental, hearing and vision are also covered, and participants are even offered free transportation to doctor and therapy appointments. Clearly a fabulous, all-inclusive program.

Do not be envious if you do not qualify, though. The income and resource (savings) requirements are harsh. The guidelines say that a person of family must have an income not exceeding 100% of the federal poverty level (**FPL**) in order to qualify for full Medicaid, and thus the D-SNP programs. This is a brutal cutoff. The Census Bureau defines the poverty guideline at a very low level each year; for 2018, it is set at **$12,140 per year for a single person, and $16,460 for a married couple**. Dependents add $4,320 to this, per person.

The $1,032 per month single/$1,391 married levels we referenced above include an extra ~$20 per month adjustment, and require maximum near-cash resources of $2,000 and $3,000 respectively, to get into Medicaid. (In Alaska and Hawaii, the figures are somewhat higher, by about 20% and 13% respectively.)

Think about that for a moment. First, in our in-the-field experience, those who qualify tend to fall much lower than even these survival levels; the number of retirees who have worked very hard at minimum wage +/- jobs for 40 or 50 years, receiving Social Security checks of $600 to $800 or so is appalling. A tiny 1-bedroom apartment in the worst area of any town is going to cost ~$400/mo., much more in many areas. How they survive, with the tiny difference being all that's available to cover food, heat, electric, clothing, furnishings, etc., seems a mathematical impossibility. Yet they do.

At least all of their medical costs are covered by the social safety nets. The correlation between poverty and multiple chronic diseases late in life is extremely high, and often the costs without these programs would exceed total income 3 or 4 fold.

The even larger tragedy that we see playing out often is in families who exceed these income limits only slightly, but who do not therefore qualify for dual Medicare/Medicaid programs.

An all-too-frequent example we see includes married couples, both worn out from 4 or 5 decades of multiple near-minimum wage jobs, both sickly, and each earning ~$700 to $800/mo. from Social Security. If they were only living together unmarried, both would qualify for D-SNP coverage, and could maintain their health, at least, at the best levels possible.

But being married, at best only one of them can qualify, because if their incomes are combined, they exceed the frightfully low limit of $1,391/month. We have seen instances where only one person has gained approval for Medicaid, whether that is by the strict application of the rule or not. If they are equally sick, which one sacrifices his or her wellbeing for their spouse?

This situation can lead to divorce being the only possible solution for a long-married, loving couple. Being single increases the qualification threshold by almost 50%, per partner. And that is a sad commentary on the state of this system.

Medical Spend-down to Qualify on Income

In most states, past or ongoing medical bills can be used to offset a portion of gross income. In cases where the person's income is just above the limits, or where medical costs are very large, this can be a lifesaver. Contact you local social services office to determine the rules in your area.

Dual-eligible beneficiaries are poorer and have more medical needs than beneficiaries who are not dually eligible. They are more likely than other Medicare beneficiaries to be frail, live with multiple chronic conditions, and have functional and cognitive impairments. According to Medicare.gov, four in 10 dual-eligible beneficiaries (39%) are under age 65 and living with disabilities, compared to about one in 10 (11%) non-dual eligible beneficiaries. A larger share of dual-eligible beneficiaries than non-dual eligible beneficiaries have three or more chronic conditions (70% versus 63%); more than half (56%) of all dual-eligible beneficiaries have a cognitive or mental impairment, compared to one quarter (25%) of non-dual eligible beneficiaries; and more than half (55%) live with one or more functional impairments in activities of daily living (**ADL**s), compared to 29 percent of other Medicare beneficiaries.

The older we get, the more likely we all are to become Dual Eligible, as our health deteriorates, and our assets get depleted.

A much greater share of dual-eligible beneficiaries than other Medicare beneficiaries live in **long-term care** facility settings (17% versus 2%). In total, about one in five Medicare beneficiaries also had Medicaid coverage in 2016. Most dual-eligible beneficiaries qualify for full Medicaid benefits, including long-term care.

Dual eligibility, and subsidized nursing home care, have become the Long Term Care insurance of America's middle class. The high cost of LTC insurance puts it out of reach for most families. The industry has struggled for years to come up with viable products at affordable prices, but has found the task difficult.

Some newer products focus on long-term Home Health Care (**HHC**) as a more affordable alternative, which is also more desirable for those who fear ending their days in a nursing home.

Lacking access to alternatives like long-term care insurance, most people pay out of their own pockets for long-term care until they have depleted their assets enough to become eligible for Medicaid.

BEWARE OF THE TRAP!

Missing out on important subsidies you qualify for

Medicaid Spend-down for Nursing Home Care

The rules are different for spending down income and assets to get to the point where Medicaid will step in for LTC. In determining how a Medicaid applicant's income affects his or her eligibility for nursing home coverage, most states use what is known as the "medically needy" or "spend-down" approach. These states allow the applicant to spend down their income on their care until they reach the state's income standard for eligibility, at which point Medicaid will begin covering their care. In this way, those with incomes that exceed Medicaid's thresholds can still qualify if they have high medical expenses, assuming they meet Medicaid's other requirements.

For families with substantial assets, especially with one member of a couple very ill and the other needing those assets for a potentially long life, spend-down gets very complicated.

In the 80s and 90s, many well-off middle aged families, seeing the freight train of long term care asset depletion approaching, utilized strategies like Medicaid-Qualifying Trusts to place some assets out of reach of the spend-down process. By 2006, congress had stepped in to make such transfers very difficult. They created laws that broke through such trusts, and even made the giving of advice for how to protect assets from depletion illegal, in and of itself.

What we are left with is a system where any transfer of assets to any other person or entity within five years of needing to enter a nursing home can be used against that person to deny care. The idea is apparently to make the outcome so barbaric that whomever assets were transferred to would be made to feel so guilty that they would "cough up" the money to avoid the person's brutal demise.

Estate planning by asset transfer is still possible, but it must be put in place FAR before any such event, and only with excellent legal and financial advice. The laws are complex and full of traps, so an experienced elder care lawyer is an absolute requirement, if assets are substantial.

In order to qualify for Medicaid, a nursing home resident's income must not be above a certain level. Most states allow individuals to spend down their excess income on their care until they reach the state's income standard. But other states impose an "income cap," which means no spend-down is allowed.

In "income cap" states, a nursing home resident won't be eligible for Medicaid if the resident's income exceeds $2,250 a month (for 2018), unless the excess income above this amount is paid into a special trust, called a "Miller" trust or a "Qualified Income Trust." The income cap states as of today are: Alabama, Alaska, Arizona, Arkansas, Colorado, Delaware, Florida, Georgia, Idaho, Indiana, Iowa, Kentucky, Louisiana, Mississippi, Nevada, New Mexico, New Jersey, Oklahoma, Oregon, South Carolina, South Dakota, Tennessee, Texas, and Wyoming.

The basic Medicaid rule for nursing home residents is that they must pay all of their income, minus certain deductions, to the nursing home. The deductions include a $60-a-month personal needs allowance (this amount may be somewhat higher or lower in your state), a deduction for any uncovered medical costs (including medical insurance premiums), and, in the case of a married applicant, an allowance for the spouse who continues to live at home if he or she needs income support. A deduction may also be allowed for a dependent child living at home.

If your situation suggests that there will be assets left in an estate after the death of the LTC patient, be aware that the state will probably try to scoop them up to repay the Medicaid costs. Talk to an estate planning advisor / attorney while there is time to take countermeasures.

A great many of us have an extended nursing home stay in our (hopefully distant) future. If we lack the resources to secure private long term care or home health care insurance, we will probably live out our days as Dual Eligibles, using a form of public assistance for probably the first time in our lives.

If you can afford the premiums to avoid it, do so. If you can't avoid it, embrace it. You won't be living in a home with theatres and gourmet meals, but you need not be in a hell hole either. The rules have changed for the better since the 90s in some ways, too.

We'll leave this subject with an update on nursing home myths:

10 Common Nursing Home Myths and Realities

Myth: Medicaid does not pay for the service you want.

Reality: Medicaid residents are entitled to the same service as other residents.

Myth: Only staff can determine the care you receive.

Reality: Residents and family have the right to participate in developing a care plan.

Myth: Staff cannot accommodate individual schedules.

Reality: A nursing home must make reasonable adjustments to honor residents' needs and preferences.

Myth: You need to hire private help.

Reality: A nursing home must provide all necessary care.

Myth: Restraints are required to prevent the resident from wandering away.

Reality: Restraints, either physical or chemical, cannot be used for the nursing home's convenience or as a form of discipline.

Myth: Family visiting hours are restricted.

Reality: Family members can visit at any time of day or night.

Myth: Therapy must be discontinued because the resident is not progressing.

Reality: Therapy may be appropriate even if resident is not progressing; Medicare may pay even without current progress.

Myth: You must pay any amount set by the nursing home for extra charges.

Reality: A nursing home may only require extra charges authorized in the admission agreement.

Myth: The nursing home has no available space for residents or family members to meet.

Reality: A nursing home must provide a private space for resident or family councils.

Myth: The resident can be evicted because he

or she is difficult or is refusing medical treatment.

Reality: Being difficult or refusing treatment does not justify eviction.

Source: "Twenty Common Nursing Home Problems and the Laws to Resolve Them" by Eric Carlson, J.D. Originally published in Clearinghouse Review Journal of Poverty Law and Policy, January/February 2006 39(910):51933

Chapter 8

Other Low-Income Programs: LIS, Extra Help and PACE

You automatically qualify for Extra Help if you have Medicare and meet any of these conditions:

- Have full Medicaid coverage.
- Get help from your state Medicaid program paying your Part B premiums (from a Medicare Savings Program)
- Get Supplemental Security Income (SSI) benefits.

As we've seen, getting qualified for Medicaid is quite difficult, and restricted to those with extreme need and few resources. What is available if you can't quite qualify?

Other programs with various names at the state and federal level offer some help up to those earning generally up to 150% of the Federal Poverty Level, with great variability on qualifications and benefit amounts.

In **Maryland**, for example, a program called SPDAP qualifes income all the way up to 300% of the FPL.

In **New Jersey**, PAAD allows 225% of FPL.

Delaware's DPAP covers you up to 200% of FPL.

It is very important for you to check what is available in your state! These programs seem to blink on and off frequently, subject to the whims and constraints of each state's budgeting process on an almost year-to-year basis.

In the Reference section of this book, we have provided some additional information, complied by the National Conference of State Legislatures. Going through the state-by-state analysis is well beyond the scope of this book, as you will see if you visit their website, at www.NCSL.org

Contact your Medicaid office or your State Health Insurance Assistance Program (SHIP) for more information. Remember, you can reapply for Extra Help at any time if your income and resources change.

Federal "Extra Help"

If you meet certain income and resource limits, you may qualify for Extra Help from Medicare to pay the costs of Medicare prescription drug coverage.

In 2018, costs are no more than $3.35 for each generic/$8.35 for each brand-name covered drug if fully qualified.

Other people pay only a portion of their Medicare drug plan premiums and deductibles based on their income level.

In 2018, you can qualify if you have up to **$18,210** in yearly income (**$24,690** for a married couple) and up to $13,820 in resources ($27,690 for a married couple).

Countable resources include:

- Money in a checking or savings account
- Stocks
- Bonds

Countable resources don't include:

- Your home
- One car
- Burial plot
- Up to $1,500 for burial expenses if you have

put that money aside

- Furniture
- Other household and personal items

Even if you automatically qualify this year, you may not qualify for Extra Help next year. Changes in your income or resources may cause you no longer to qualify for one of the programs listed above. You'll get a notice from Medicare (on grey paper) by the end of September if you no longer automatically qualify. Even if you get this notice, you may still qualify, but you need to apply to find out.

If your co-payment amounts change next year, you'll get a notice (on orange paper) in the mail in early October with the new amounts.

If you don't get a notice from Medicare, you'll get the same level of Extra Help that you got for this year.

Paying the right amount

If you're not sure if you're paying the right amount, call your drug plan. Your plan may ask you to give information to help them check the level of Extra Help you should get. Get your plan's contact information from a Personalized Search (under General Search), or search by plan name.

If you paid for prescriptions since you qualified for Extra Help and you aren't enrolled in a Medicare drug plan, you may be able to get some money back. Keep your receipts, and call your plan. Or, you can contact Medicare's Limited Income Newly Eligible Transition (NET) Program at 1-800-783-1307 for more information (TTY: 711).

Other ways to lower your prescription drug costs

- Look into generic drugs. Ask your doctor if there are generics that will work as well as your current brand-name drugs.
- Ask your doctor about less expensive brand-name drugs.
- Consider using mail-order pharmacies.
- Use the Medicare Plan Finder to compare Medicare drug plans to find a plan with lower costs.
- Find out if your state offers help paying for drug costs.
- Find out if the company that makes your drug offers help paying for it.

Categories of Federal-level Extra Help

If you qualify for "full" Extra Help, you receive coverage throughout the year (no doughnut hole), pay no premium or deductible, and pay very little for your prescriptions. If you qualify for "partial" Extra Help, you receive coverage throughout the year and pay a reduced premium and deductible and as little as 15 percent of the cost of your drugs.

Here are the current limits and benefits under the four levels of Extra Help for 2018:

Level 1: If you receive full Medicaid benefits and live in a nursing home, you automatically qualify for full Extra Help and pay nothing for your prescription drugs coverage – no premiums, deductibles or copays.

Level 2: If you receive Medicaid or Supplemental Security Income (SSI) or if your state pays your Medicare premiums, you automatically qualify for full Extra Help. You pay no premium or deductible for Medicare drug coverage. Depending on your income, your copays for each prescription in 2017, copays are $1.20 or $3.70 for generics; $3.70 or $8.25 for brand names and nothing for catastrophic coverage.

Level 3: If your current income is no higher than **$1,357** a month (single) or **$1,827** a month (for a married couple living together), and your assets (mainly savings) are no more than $8,780 (single) or $13,930 (married), you pay no premium or deductible. Your copays for each prescription are:

$2.95 for generic drugs, $7.40 for brand-name drugs and nothing for catastrophic coverage.

Level 4: If your current income is no higher than **$1,508** a month (single) or **$2,030** a month (for a married couple living together), and your assets (mainly savings) are no more than $13,640 (single) or $27,250 (married), you pay a percentage of your plan's premium depending on income. You also pay: an annual deductible ($82 in 2017); and no more than 15 percent of the cost of each prescription. At the catastrophic level of coverage you pay $2.95 for generics and $7.40 for brand-name drugs in 2016 ($3.30 and $8.25 respectively in 2017) or 5 percent of the cost, whichever is greater. (The asset limits above include $1,500 per person for intended funeral expenses, whether or not you've set aside money for this purpose.)

Low Income Subsidy (LIS) privileges

Note that qualifying for any level of extra help is considered **LIS** privileged, and carries another important benefit: **You are permitted to enroll/disenroll from any PDP or Medicare Advantage MA-PD at any time during the year.** You are not restricted to the Annual Election Period from October 15th to December 7th. This give you much greater flexibility in securing the lowest possible cost for the drugs you need.

In some areas, it is possible to qualify for some level of state-based LIS with income as high as 300% of the Federal Poverty Level, over $3,000/month for a single individual. Google <your state> <low income healthcare subsidy> for detailed hits that you can start to whittle down.

Program of All-Inclusive Care for the Elderly (PACE)

The Programs of All-Inclusive Care for the Elderly (PACE) provides comprehensive medical and social services to certain frail, community-dwelling elderly individuals, most of whom are dually eligible for Medicare and Medicaid benefits. A team of health professionals provides PACE participants with coordinated care.

For most participants, the comprehensive service package enables them to remain in the community rather than receive care in a nursing home. Among the 30+ states with active PACE programs, more than **90%** of the participants are able to receive their care in their family home, saving money for the healthcare programs, while giving the seniors their preferred living environment.

Financing for the program is capped, which allows providers to deliver all services participants need rather than only those reimbursable under

Medicare and Medicaid fee-for-service plans. PACE is a program under Medicare, and states can elect to provide PACE services to Medicaid beneficiaries as an optional Medicaid benefit. The PACE program becomes the sole source of Medicaid and Medicare benefits for PACE participants.

PACE Eligibility

Individuals can join PACE if they meet certain conditions:

- Age 55 or older
- Live in the service area of a PACE organization
- Eligible for nursing home care
- Be able to live safely in the community

The PACE program becomes the sole source of services for Medicare and Medicaid eligible enrollees. Individuals can leave the program at any time. See Medicaid.gov for more information.

PART II

Matching Your Limitations to the Maze

Chapter 9

How to Decide Your Strategy

"A goal, properly set, is halfway reached."
– Abraham Lincoln

We all have our own specific limitations, and our own special capabilities.

Winning the best outcome from Medicare requires internalizing a lesson from the Dirty Harry School of Life. As Clint Eastwood famously said, "A man has got to know his limitations." (So does a woman.)

You will need to gain a clear understanding of the major factors influencing your new future as a Senior Citizen, and you must force yourself to analyze your life prospects as they really are now, and as they are likely to change as you grow ever closer to the eternal celestial dirt-nap. How you thought your retirement would be when you were 30 or 40 or 50 has certainly changed over time, but most of us still color our perceptions of self through the memories of youthful endurance and unlimited possibilities. This automatic optimism has no bearing on your current reality, which is what you must clear-headedly examine.

BEWARE OF THE TRAP!

Choosing a plan because a friend likes it

The two most important aspects of your life, for this purpose, are ***your health*** and ***your finances***.

Take a hard look at your real state of health. Do you still exercise as regularly and as energetically as you know you should, or are the missed workouts starting to become the norm?

How much has your endurance slipped? What aches and pains have crept up on you? How frequently do you visit a doctor? How many pills do you take? Have you noticed an increased susceptibility to colds, flus, infections?

Think carefully about how these characteristics have changed for you over the years, and try to picture each of them as a *trend*, or as a line on a graph.

I f you feel your health is excellent, for example, you might get a mental picture like this:

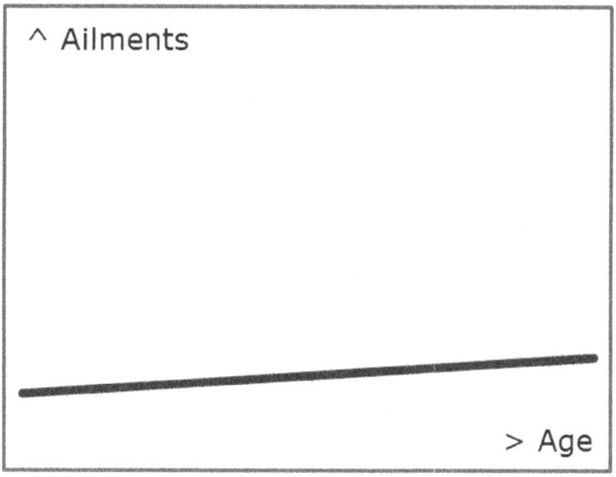

If you're feeling not-so-well, it might look like this:

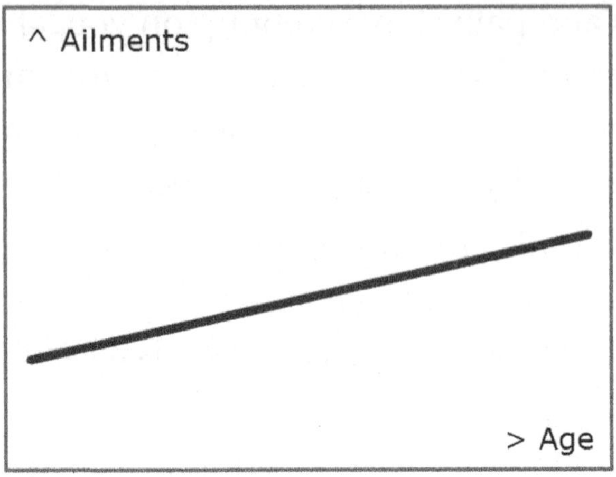

Looking past the crude artwork, what do both of these trendlines have in common?

They are both *linear*. That is, trending (upward), at a constant slope, or rate of change. Which is, after all, how the human brain tends to project trends. We instinctively look at our impression of the past, and project it forward in time, linearly. But that isn't the way life works.

Change is sporadic, unpredictable in nature. If you've ever followed the stock market or mutual funds, you know well that "past results are not predictive of future returns." Stock prices are random in the short term, generally rising over long periods of time, but *nothing* is guaranteed.

But for a chart of Ailments, we can know the endpoint with certainty. Death gets us all. Usually after a period of severely declining health.

And that means that any trend projected straight-line, in the case of health, will be wrong — except for the few of us that die suddenly, without any prior warning. For those , Medicare won't matter...

This is a more accurate picture of our health problems as we age:

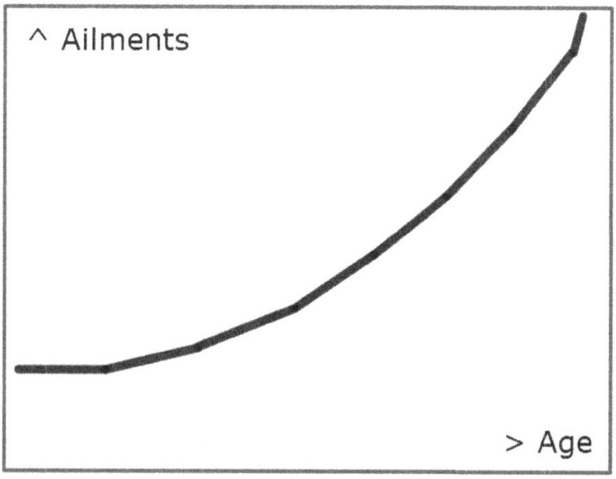

At some point, our problems become exponential, and we go off the chart — to the great beyond.

Keep this in the front of your mind as you try to project what your remaining years may look like, healthwise. No matter how much you want to avoid such thoughts.

Now take the same kind of a hard look at your finances. For most of us, regardless how much we tried to be thoughtful and prepared for retirement, our Social Security checks and pension income are a tough reality. Our pocketbooks barely survive until the next month's refill. If you prepared better than most, and maybe had a little extra luck pushing you along the way, you may get a rough plot of your future finances something like this:

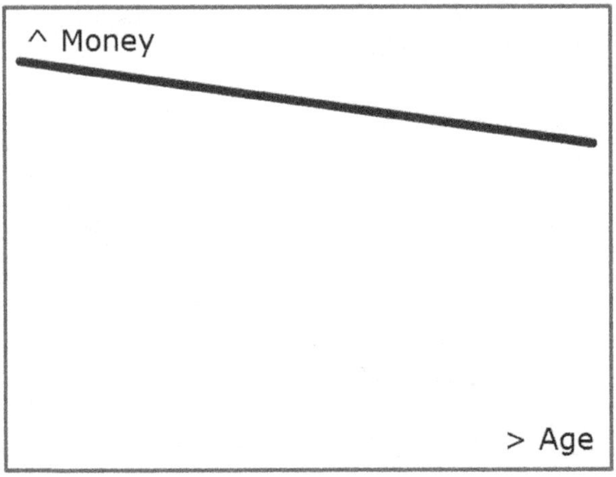

In other words, plenty now, still fine for a long time, and plenty left over at the end for your heirs or your favorite causes. Pat yourself on the back. Its well earned, for you've done a great job. Be content that you are well within the top 10% of retirees!

If your financial fortunes have been less propitious, perhaps you'd paint a line more like this:

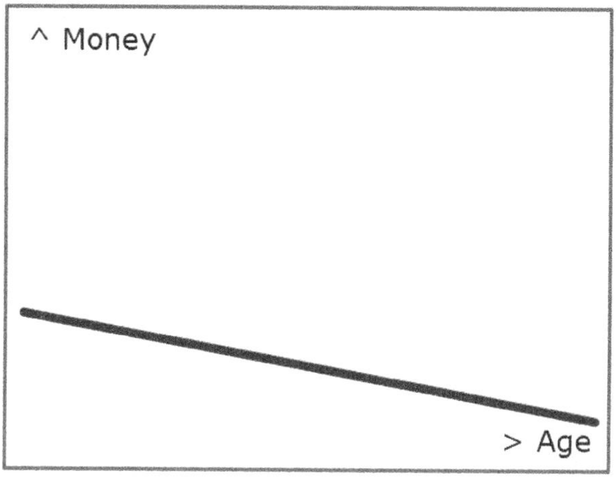

Many, many seniors find themselves facing this kind of scary picture.

If you were among those readers who most recognized the second depiction for Ailments, above, you are more than *four times* as likely to pick this Money projection as one you can identify with. Poor health and poor finances are very strongly correlated. Whether it is because lack of good health led to financial misfortune, or strained finances led to poor healthcare and resulting chronic problems, the cause/effect matters little. You face special challenges in retirement.

The great news for you, as we have just seen, is that the American system has numerous safeguards built in, designed specifically for those in the aging community with limited means. In fact, most of our readers at the lower end of the income/assets scale will be able to qualify for the many special programs that provide more and better medical benefits, with fewer drawbacks, than many of our middle-income readers.

If you thought that your financial situation was between these two depictions, you are among the highest percentage of our readers. You have enough income and assets to be comfortable now, and you feel that your future path should be OK, if not fabulous.

Your choices must continue to be smart and well-informed. You will not have the safety net of social programs provided for the neediest seniors, and you will certainly not have the luxury of correcting poor lifestyle or healthcare choices by throwing money at the fixes. To maintain your health as you would probably prefer, you will need to focus more on protecting your exposures proactively.

Your strategy should be focused on limiting risk to the assets and lifestyle you have accumulated as much as possible. You must also gain a clear picture of how your future finances will not project a gently sloping linear decline, but are far more likely to decrease at an increasing rate as you deal with life's realities in older age.

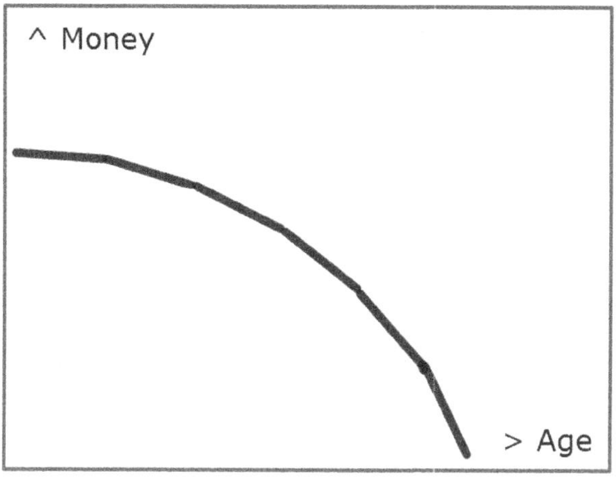

Negative health surprises are, by far, the most profound cause of unpredictable hits to your wealth. Your best preparation involves anticipating as many of the possible exposures as possible, and budgeting for them in advance. To the extent that insurance products are available to you, and can be coordinated in ways that make sense to your personal risk tolerance, you will find yourself a more focused consumer of insurance than at any prior time of your life.

You will want to allocate a bearable portion of your comfortable fixed income to counter your unknowable health surprises, and it will be a higher portion than you like. You will also want to take steps to avoid the **nightmare scenario** -- running out of money before you run out of time.

Now that you have a new focus on your future health and expected money, let's see how this information can lead you to the best personal strategy for making your Medicare choices.

We will look at this from the two most extreme ends. As we do so, actively try to see where your family fits on the spectrum of possibilities. You will find that your decisions have now been greatly simplified.

Chapter 10

If Your Health is the Bigger Limitation...

...we are going to assume the converse — that your income is not terribly limited, if you see yourself in this category.

You will want the greatest choice in providers and institutions to care for your health problems, and *assuming we are talking about your initial enrollment period within 6 months of turning 65 and getting Part B*, your acceptance is guaranteed at the lowest prices. Medigap is accepted by virtually every doctor and hospital, though the very best will have surcharges. Should your health further deteriorate, and you find yourself in need of exceptional care, Medigap is by far your best option.

Refer back to the charts in Chapter 5, and our discussion of Plan selection vs. prices. If you want the maximum coverage, Plan F has it — but only until 1/1/2020. After that date, people who already have F will be able to maintain it, but may experience faster rate hikes than other plans, because 1) insurers may try to take advantage of a semi-captive market, and 2) the F member pool will age faster than those still accepting new 65 year olds, resulting in an older, more expensive group over time.

Good alternatives are Plans G and N, making you pay the first $183 per year, plus excess charges if you choose both N and providers who do not accept assignment. The pools of both of these will continue to be refreshed by new 65 year olds, so the premium increases should be lower than for F.

Study the pricing and rate hike trends in your area with your agent, and pick one of those 3.

Next, you will definitely need add-ons to fill the gaps left by the Plan you select. Look again at the table of Pros and Cons in Chapter 6.

Remember that Medigap supplements do not include a number of important coverages, including:

- **Prescription drugs!**
- Dental
- Vision
- Chiropractic
- Hearing

- Podiatry
- Long Term Care

This is so because the various letter-defined Plans are standardized by law, and they are designed only to fill in the "gaps" in Medicare coverage created by deductibles, co-pays, and coinsurance (NONinsurance). If Original Medicare does not cover a category, Medigap policies **cannot** cover it either — thus the long list above.

Medicare Advantage plans are not confined by the strict standardization of Medigap. They are required to provide at least the coverages of OM, but permitted to add more. In the competition for members, plans add extra benefits they know will be attractive to consumers. Inexpensive extras are common, including gym memberships, 24-hour nurse lines, chiropractic and foot care, vision, and preventive dental. These extras are usually fairly limited, with significant co-pays, but they are great marketing tools.

As you might imagine, numerous insurance companies have stepped in with products to fill these "Medigap-gaps", and you will need to determine which are important enough for you to add to your protection.

One of these coverages you should think of as a *requirement* is a stand-alone Prescription Drug

Plan (PDP). It really is not optional, if your objective is to cover your financial exposure to your health issues as well as possible. These plans are relatively inexpensive, ranging from about $20 per month to over $60/mo., depending on what you want in terms of deductibles and co-pays, and which plans cover your specific drugs. Medicare.gov has a very good drug list comparison engine, and your agent will be able to generate pointed comparisons for you as well.

After a PDP, the most common add-on products are Dental and Vision. Preventive-care-only dental plans are cheap, but do not cover costs of dentures, root canals, crowns etc. Plans to cover these items are available, but at significantly greater costs, and with annual limitations. Vision care is normally an inexpensive add-on.

So make sure your choices are easily within your budget, and then relax! You have provided yourself with something between the Cadillac and the Mercedes of senior healthcare plans.

Chapter 11

If your Income is the Bigger Limitation

Take another look at your income stream as it is likely to be after full retirement, and ask yourself this question: *can I be happy with the lifestyle that would result if I spent $____ per month on healthcare?*

The number to fill in the blank is the amount it would cost for a Medigap Supplement Plan G or N (see the back of Chapter 5 for ranges), plus a Prescription Drug Plan and the co-pays for what drugs you're likely to need, for the next 20 years or so.

The Medigap premium is more predictable than the drug costs, and 20 years is a long time. But if you take the current costs and double them, that is a starting point. For a single man aged 65, try $500/mo as a start. Single woman, 65, perhaps $400. Add them together if you're a married couple.

If those numbers leave you with a comfortable lifestyle, your lowest-risk alternative is still the Medigap Supplement and PDP. They cover your major exposures and are budgetable, and you retain full freedom of choice of providers.

If you could not live with that level of monthly spend for a long time, you still have some great choices. They will come from the second universe of products and programs, Medicare Advantage ("Part C").

You will very likely be able to find a low to $0 premium Medicare Advantage plan with prescription drugs included (MA-PD). But you will need to put extra money away diligently for the day when you have to pay the deductibles, co-pays and coinsurance that your plan still leaves to you.

You will need to choose care providers from within the network of the plan you choose, unless you are willing to pay much higher out-of-pocket costs. Even if you stay entirely within network, your MaxOOP could be $4,000 to $6,700 in a bad year, depending on the plan.

You can reduce this exposure significantly with added insurance products, like hospital indemnity or dread disease coverage, but your risk will still be greater than with a solid Medigap/PDP combination.

So you have to weigh the options if you are in

the grey area, where either path is possible. If the monthly outlay is impossible, or unacceptably damaging to your lifestyle, MA-PD is the obvious choice.

BEWARE OF THE TRAP!

Missing the "power shift" -- failing to realize that a lower-than-expected fixed income changes everything – about how you've judged cost vs. risk in the past

Consider carefully what you're tempted to call unacceptable in regard to your lifestyle.

The decision to reject the potential full coverage of a Medigap supplement plan can be irreversible. If you acquire any one of a great many survivable conditions (like angina, A-fib, any kind of cancer, rheumatoid arthritis, pancreatitis, chronic bronchitis, hepatitis, diabetes requiring insulin, even clinical depression, and many, many more), you may be rejected if you later apply for Medigap.

Your guaranteed-issue (no medical questions) periods to acquire Medigap are very limited — basically the 6 months after you turn 65, or within 1 year of first starting on a Medicare Advantage plan and electing to change to Medigap (trial right).

If you choose Medicare Advantage, look for a plan that includes a prescription drug element (MA-PD), with the best combination of a low (or zero) monthly premium, a low MaxOOP, and a high level of extra benefits, like dental and vision coverage.

If you plan to travel, or if travel for more than a week or so in the future is a real possibility, you **must** get an MA-PD plan that is a **PPO**, not an HMO, or you could find yourself without any coverage at all (other than legitimate emergency room items) when away from home. The difference will likely cost you $30 to $60 per month.

Make sure that your primary physician is a member of the network, as well as any specialists you see.

Check every drug you take against the formulary for the plan, and add up the co-pays and deductibles you will have to pay.

Make sure you will be able to afford the specific co-pays and NONinsurance for any treatments or tests you are likely to need.

Plan on spending a day or so on the Medicare.gov website, doing your research, and picking a plan. Better yet, contact an independent agent or broker who is a Medicare specialist to guide you through the process.

Try to keep aside the money you save monthly on premiums for unexpected costs in the future. If your assets begin to dwindle dangerously, study Chapters 7 and 8, and plan for your safety net. The option of qualifying as a Dual Eligible will be there for you if you need it, and as we've seen, it is comprehensive assistance.

Chapter 12

Achieving Maximum Predictability

If you financial situation is somewhat comfortable, you may want to look at a variety of options for covering your additional exposures. While you cannot be prepared for every single possibility, you can "seal the vault" against the most likely invaders. Let's first look at supplemental health insurance.

What Is Supplemental Health Insurance?

Supplemental health insurance is any healthcare plan that gives you additional coverage beyond the minimum medical coverage. For example, supplemental health policies can provide coverage for things like dental, vision, hearing, critical illness, long-term care, cancer and other dread diseases, short-term care, accidental death or dismemberment, and more. These supplemental health insurance plans help pay the costs of medical expenses that are not covered by basic insurance plans. They also help with expenses accrued from copays, coinsurance, and deductibles.

Dental, Vision & Hearing

These three commonly needed medical services are not covered at all by Medicare, nor by Medigap supplements. Some limited coverage may be included with Medicare Advantage plans, at the option of the carrier.

Separately purchased dental coverage is usually limited to preventative care, at least in the first year or two of a policy. Only after a period of time paying premiums will even higher priced plans cover major services, like crowns, dentures or root canals. These plans can be thought of almost like discount programs, because most people buy them when they are already contemplating some dental work. Immediate or high-dollar coverage is thus expensive.

Vision and hearing policies are similar, though not as expensive.

Hospital Indemnity

Hospital Indemnity insurance pays you a fixed dollar amount for every day you spend in a hospital, in addition to all other coverages. This money is paid directly to you, to cover indirect losses like travel, loss of income, costs for a companion, etc.

Long Term Care/Home Health Care

These policies cover required care outside of a hospital, as defined and capped by the policy. The coverage is usually limited by a daily maximum benefit. The specifics of what a plan will and won't cover are variable and complex, so be sure you know what you are buying. A good agent, who is very familiar with all of your other coverages, is essential if you are considering this.

Dread Disease

Cancer, Heart Attack and Stroke are the three biggest killer diseases we have. Policies are available for each of them individually, or as combined coverage.

These policies typically pay out a specified face amount upon diagnosis of the ailment(s) specified. This is paid in addition to other health insurance coverages, directly to the policy owner or beneficiary, similar to hospital indemnity.

It is common to see policies offered with a large number of available additional coverages, known as **riders**. Examples include cancer recurrence, heart and stroke restoration, intensive care indemnity, return of premium upon death, etc. Again, a good agent is essential to explain and guide you to the best and most likely payout benefits.

These policies are especially appealing if you have a strong family history of the covered diseases striking your close family members. A large check can greatly ease the pain of a horrible diagnosis.

Life Insurance Add-ons

It is also possible to get some of the above benefits as riders to life insurance policies, including whole life policies bought to cover final expenses.

A final expense policy is bought not to cover your own risks, but those of your loved ones when you pass. Funerals are very expensive affairs, and the family you leave behind will want to honor you as much as they can afford — even if it means doing so with a credit card that may take a decade to pay off.

But the policies to avoid those problems for your family can provide you direct benefits, as well. With a living benefits rider, a specified portion of the face amount will be paid directly to you upon diagnosis of a terminal illness. This makes it functionally similar to a dread disease policy.

AD&D

Accidental Death and Dismemberment policies pay a stated fixed benefit upon the loss of a limb or blindness, as well as if the insured dies as the result of an accident not of his or her own causation. They are typically seen as part of employer benefit packages, and not often purchased individually, except as riders to a life policy.

When Combined With Medigap Supplements

Look again at the Pros vs. Cons list in Chapter 6. Thinking in terms of a Medigap Plan F, which covers every one of Medicare's "gaps", there are still holes to patch.

The one gap you must fill is a part D Prescription Drug Plan. Not doing so leaves you exposed to great cost, and also incurs a penalty for every month you delay, without creditable coverage.

Next, the most commonly used are dental and vision, with no coverage by Medicare or Medigap. Coverage can be bought from a different carrier, usually for little expense.

The big, expensive risks are covered by the Medigap.

When Combined With Medicare Advantage

MA and even MA-PD plans, as we have seen, leave you exposed to the big, expensive risks, up to the MaxOOP of the plan you get. You have substantial co-pays for tests and hospital stays, and you have to pay the 20% NONinsurance for Part B services. Your co-pays for doctors' visits are small, but can add up in a bad year.

The legal limit for this amount, as long as you get all of your care within the network, is $6,700 per year. Some plans set MaxOOP as low as $4,000/year, but these will carry a monthly premium that is not $0 (but usually well less than $100). It depends on what is available in your area.

So how do you cover the potential OOP? One way is to save for it, from the savings you have from not buying Medigap. You need discipline, and enough luck not to get really sick in the first few years.

Another possibility is to consider some form of indemnity coverage, either dread disease or hospital. But this only makes sense if the cost is well less than the Medigap alternative you would otherwise select.

Chapter 13

Getting the Care You Need from the Bureaucracy

Your PCP

Your primary care provider is perhaps the most important person to you, for seeing that "the system" does not overrun your rights to excellent care.

He or she should be your greatest advocate when your health plan, or Medicare itself, try to deny you drugs or treatments that your PCP believes are necessary for you. The first step after any denial is usually a letter from your doctor, giving reasons why a decision should be reversed.

This seems like a silly waste of precious physician's time and resources. But it has become an embedded reality of a system where clinicians' decisions about treatment are continually second-guessed by administrators and legions of bureaucrats. Your doctor hates it too, but he or she is used to it by now, and prepared for the extra paperwork.

Most denials, well over 50%, get reversed if the PCP or patient takes the time and effort to complain. The process will usually start with you voicing an objection, though often the physician will initiate it on their own.

If your provider does not seem to want to take the extra effort when you feel strongly that he or she should, it might be time to find a better provider.

"Grievance" with your plan provider

Technically, this is a complaint about the way your Medicare health plan or Medicare drug plan is giving care. For example, you may file a grievance if you have a problem calling the plan or if you're unhappy with the way a staff person at the plan has behaved towards you. However, if you have a complaint about a plan's refusal to cover a service, supply, or prescription, you file an appeal.

However, this is the **power term** to use when speaking to your private insurer customer service center about **any problem or coverage decision**, as you simultaneously request escalation of your call to a Supervisor.

This term gets their attention quickly, as it implies that your matter is about to be referred directly to CMS, making management not only aware of the issue, but forced to respond quickly to a summons from a higher authority. Which is of course the last thing they want.

Invoking this term triggers the dislike of bureaucracy in the people you need to grant you a favorable decision. You turn the tables, because they now face the wall of process and procedure just like you, at an even higher stress level.

Your complaint may be more properly handled by a Appeal, but that term fails to produce the emotional reaction in the customer service staff that may lead to an immediate reversal. A formal appeal is the next step.

Key tip

Should you ever need to talk directly to Medicare, here is a tip that will save you hours of frustration in the call canter queue:

Call at night.

1-800-MEDICARE is open 24 hours, 365 days a year. They never close. Very few people seem to know this, and it produces a lot of one-ring pickups after 9 or 10pm. The representatives often seem actually *eager* to talk to someone, which is quite different from busy daytime hours (especially Mondays).

Appeals

An appeal is the action you take if you disagree with a coverage or payment decision made by Medicare, your Medicare Advantage Plan (like an HMO or PPO), other Medicare health plan, or your Medicare Prescription Drug Plan.

You have the right to appeal if Medicare, your Medicare health plan, or your Medicare Prescription Drug Plan denies one of these requests:

- A request for a health care service, supply, item, or prescription drug that you think you should be able to get.
- A request for payment of a health care service, supply, item, or prescription drug you already got.
- A request to change the amount you must pay for a health care service, supply, item, or prescription drug.

You can also appeal if Medicare or your plan **stops** providing or paying for all or part of a health care service, supply, item, or prescription drug you think you still need.

The Medicare appeals process looks ominous, but the reality is that **more than 50% of appeals are**

decided in favor of the person making the appeal, and most of those reversals occur early in the process. This means that you must file an appeal if you think you have been denied proper coverage, and you have great odds of winning.

The full appeals process has 5 levels, which differ slightly depending on whether you have Original Medicare, a Medigap supplement, or Medicare Advantage, but the broad outline is as follows:

- Level 1: Redetermination by your plan, or by the Medicare Administrative Contractor (MAC) if Original Medicare
- Level 2: Reconsideration by a Qualified Independent Contractor (QIC) or an Independent Review Entity (IRE)
- Level 3: Hearing before an Administrative Law Judge (ALJ)
- Level 4: Review by the Medicare Appeals Council (Appeals Council)
- Level 5: Judicial review by a federal district court

Timelines also differ somewhat, but here is a graphic of the process if appealing a decision by your prescription drug plan:

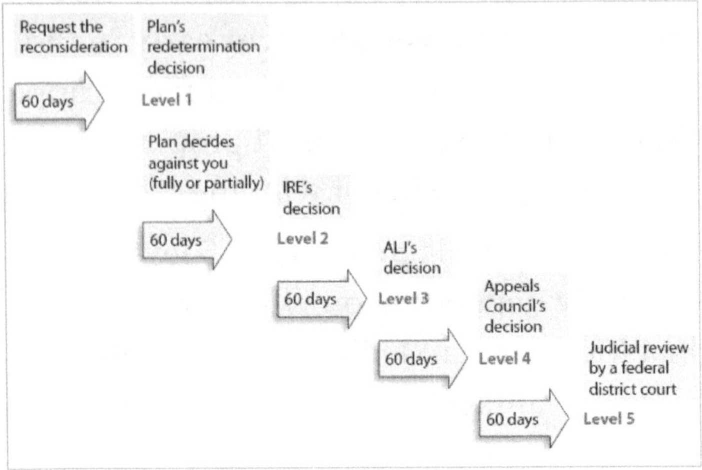

This diagram, and much of this information, is from an excellent consumer booklet put out by CMS, discussing the intricacies of the appeals process. If you ever find yourself in an appeals situation, it is required reading. Find it here:

https://www.medicare.gov/Pubs/pdf/11525.pdf

Expedited Appeals

What can you do in an urgent situation, like when you're in the hospital, and "they" give you a notice that care — or coverage -- will be discontinued?

When you're admitted as an inpatient to a hospital, you have the right to get the hospital care that's necessary to diagnose and treat your illness or injury. If you think you're being discharged from the hospital too soon, you have the right to ask your Beneficiary and Family Centered Quality Improvement Organization (BFCC-QIO)to review your case. To get the BFCC-QIO's phone number, visit Medicare.gov/contacts, or call 1-800-MEDICARE (1-800-633-4227). TTY users should call 1-877-486-2048.

Within 2 days of your admission, you should get a notice called "An Important Message from Medicare about Your Rights" (sometimes called the "Important Message from Medicare" or the "IM"). If you don't get this notice, ask for it. This notice lists the BFCC-QIO's contact information and explains:

- Your right to get all medically necessary hospital services
- Your right to be involved in any decisions that the hospital, your doctor, or anyone else makes about your hospital services and to know who will pay for them
- Your right to get the services you need after you leave the hospital
- Your right to appeal a discharge decision and the steps for appealing the decision
- The circumstances under which you will or won't have to pay for charges for continuing to stay in the hospital

- Information on your right to get a detailed notice about why your covered services are ending

If the hospital gives you the IM more than 2 days before your discharge day, it must either give you a copy of your original, signed IM or provide you with a new one (that you must sign) before you're discharged.

How do I ask for a fast appeal? You may have the right to ask the BFCC-QIO for a fast appeal. Follow the directions on the IM to request a fast appeal if you think your Medicare-covered hospital services are ending too soon.

You must ask for a fast appeal no later than the day you're scheduled to be discharged from the hospital. **If you ask for your appeal within this timeframe, you can stay in the hospital without paying for your stay (except for applicable coinsurance or deductibles) while you wait to get the decision from the BFCC-QIO.**

If you miss the deadline for a fast appeal, you can still ask the BFCC-QIO to review your case, but different rules and timeframes apply. For more information, contact the BFCC-QIO.

One other thing to watch out for regarding hospital stays: it is possible for you to be treated for several days in a hospital without being considered an "inpatient". This happens because of the reverse-incentives imposed by Medicare in the event of rapid re-admissions or items like hospital-originated infections.

BEWARE OF THE TRAP!

Do not allow a hospital to make you an "inside-outpatient" when it will impact your rights to benefits, like repeating your Part A deductible, or defeating your ability to go to a nursing home only after a three-day hospital stay

They are required to give you notice of such a determination. In this case, demand to speak to the BFCC-QIO immediately, and get vocal.

Chapter 14

If it All Goes to Hell

Even with the best-laid plans, life is full of continuous surprises. What do you do if your health and your finances both fail you at the same time?

Adapt and overcome.

If you see this situation coming from some distance, please study Chapters 7, 8, and 11 carefully. There are many programs in place to help people in this situation, and if you can identify one or more to go after, you can start the planning necessary to find out how to qualify, and to adjust what you may need to adjust before you apply.

An excellent objective would be to shoot for full Medicare/Medicaid **Dual Eligibility**, and then sign up with the Medicare Advantge plan in your area which offers the most advantageous extra benefits.

These Dual-eligible Special Needs Plans (D-SNPs) were discussed in some depth earlier, so here we will just say that some spectacular benefits are available. One plan we've seen advertised lately offers:

- $0 monthly premiums
- $0 co-pays to see your doctors
- $0 coinsurance for hospital stays
- $1.50 generic and $3.70 brand name prescription copay
- Up to $1,000 per year in free over the counter drugs, vitamins, bandages, braces, cough medicines, electric toothbrushes — almost anything you'd find in a large drug store
- Up to $2,500 per year in dental services, including major services like crowns, dentures, and oral surgery (which is very unusual)
- Vision exams and eyewear or contacts
- Hearing exams and up to $2,500 for hearing aids
- Free transportation to doctors' offices, even pharmacies
- A 24-hour access nurse line, for any reason
- Free virtual doctor visits, using your

computer or mobile device

- A free on-your-person emergency monitor, and free monthly service, for falls or other emergencies
- Outpatient substance abuse, group or individual therapy sessions
- Health club or gym membership
- Podiatric care
- Chiropractic care
- Short-term nursing home care
- Home health care

That is an amazing list of benefits at virtually **zero cost**! In addition, *because of the full Medicaid qualification, your long-term nursing home care (LTC) would be paid for by Medicaid.* Total coverage, like only our Congressmen and Senators' health plans. We'd bet that, if you are low on both money and health, this list would go a very long way towards comforting you, and relieving your financial stress too.

If medical bills and expenses have contributed to your deteriorating situation, you can use them to your advantage here to get Medicaid-qualified. Even unpaid bills can be applied to lower your gross income to a qualifying level, in the process called spend-down that we discussed earlier. Silver linings have not been abolished.

Also, take comfort in the fact that, in tough circumstances, **providers gotta provide**. They cannot turn you away in most cases.

Many of them will be willing to work with you if you explain your circumstances, and if for some reason you cannot qualify for Medicaid.

You may have to deal with collection agencies later, but they can only do so much. If your back is to the wall, often a credible threat of being forced into bankruptcy by their actions will be enough to get them off your back. And the threat will probably work as well as the actual filing, be a lot cheaper and easier, and generally a lot better for you all around.

Focus on getting better, and don't sweat the small stuff.

Collectors are always small stuff.

Chapter 15

So What Do You Do Next?

You now have the knowledge to determine for yourself the general actions you should take to best plan your future healthcare. Next is to identify the exact carriers, products, and prices.

So now, you have to make a choice:

- Go it alone, or
- Get a Broker or Independent Agent (not a captive agent with only one or two products to represent) who is appointed with several Medigap carriers **and** several Medicare Advantage carriers

When we started writing this book, we didn't really have a great plan for helping you to decide how to proceed, if you chose the latter. And we do not recommend the former.

If you go it alone, and you decide on Medicare Advantage as the crux of your plan, you can use the resources available on Medicare.gov to directly sign up for MA, MA-PD, and PDP plans. As long as you are able to gather all the important details (not shown on Medicare.gov, but available on the websites of the individual insurers linked-to there), and compare them side-by-side to come to a clear understanding of the differences, an agent is not required to sign up.

For Medigap, the capabilities of Medicare.gov are much more limited, including giving misleading and nearly meaningless annual cost comparisons. And a search of [how we calculate "estimated annual cost"] will take you to a promising, but dead, link. You can, though, use the plan search to find which insurers cover your area, and to get website addresses. But then you will need to go through each insurer's site individually — and many of them will just push you to an agent rather than give you the info you're looking for.

However, as it used to be in the travel agency business, you should know that **there is no cost to the client to use the services of a broker or independent agent**. There is no fee for drawing upon his or her expertise, and the insurance products **cost the same** whether they are bought through a broker or through any website, including Medicare.gov.

So why not avail yourself of the expertise? An experienced agent will be able to confirm that your choices are sound, and will know a great deal about the providers in your area and be able to explain subtle differences that a consumer would never notice.

For example, there are several carriers that price Medigap Plan G **much lower** than Plan N (Oxford life is one example, in certain markets). Why? Only their actuaries know for sure. The benefits of G are clearly superior to those of N. But wouldn't you like to be aware of these mispricings and market anomalies?

If you knew that it is possible to save over $40,000 over the course of your Medicare enrollment, would you be interested enough to make sure to have a knowledgeable, honest, client-focused agent on your side?

Refer back to the price comparisons we showed you in Chapter 5, with the range of costs in different locations, for the exact same standardized plan. Those ranges in each case were about $190 to $200 per month.

The SSA currently calculates the life expectancy of a 65 year old man as 84.3 years, and a woman as 86.6. Do the math: $190/month for 20 years is $45,600. That's a lot of money that could be spent for the fun things in life instead of insurance!

Also, in the world of Medicare, one certainty is that changes in programs and rules are constant, occurring at least annually. Having an agent in your corner gives you a buffer to provide notice of, and advice for dealing with, those changes.

There is only one good reason for not working with an agent: ***fear of being sold*** something disadvantageous; the ***lack of trust*** for an insurance salesman.

We understand, and share the natural aversion to salespeople's influence.

Everything considered, we still urge our readers to find a broker or independent agent worthy of your trust and confidence. Consult with him or her at whatever length you need, to arrive at a clear understanding of what products are best-suited to you, and why. Find someone who will advocate for you, someone you will feel so good about that you will spontaneously refer your best friends and family, for years to come.

But HOW can you find such a person, and get past the trust issues? We need to provide you specific answers, to fulfill the promise of this book.

In trying to supply an answer to this question, it has become very clear to us that there is a large, unfilled need in the marketplace. There is no resource for finding agents who specialize in Medicare products *and* who are licensed, qualified and appointed with several carriers representing *each* of the two universes of products. And there is no resource or strategy for answering the question of ***whom can I trust?***

So we are going to fill that void.

We are forming an association of Medicare experts, and including a set of membership requirements that should go a long way towards instilling a greater degree of trust than is otherwise likely.

It is called the American Association of Professional Medicare Advisors, AAPMA, and will be found at the new website **MedicarePros.org**

The requirements for membership are simple, but not easy. Members must:

1. Hold current state insurance licenses for all three lines of authority — Life, Health, and Medicare products
2. Hold current certifications from AHIP, the American Health Insurance Providers organization
3. Hold current appointments with ***several***

carriers for Medigap Supplement products

4. Hold current appointments and annual certs for ***several*** carriers for Medicare Advantage products
5. Commit to a Pledge of Ethics that holds the interests of the client above the interests of the member, promising to *always* ***search for and obtain*** *the best combination of low price and stability to fit each individual clients' needs.*

This last item is very important. It means that members will seek very low prices for their clients, even if that means doing the extra administrative work required to take on a new carrier, if that's what it takes to deliver the best value to just one customer.

This is not a common practice in the insurance industry, but we take it upon ourselves willingly. Being committed to the highest levels of client service means doing a lot of extra work that most agents will not do. It is far easier to just take a product "off the shelf" of an agent's current list of carriers than it is to take on a new contract, just to save one client a few dollars per month.

We will seek out members who go the extra mile. As a famous coach once said, "there are no traffic jams on the extra mile." Clients love it.

We believe that there are a great many Medicare specialists who behave this way **naturally**, and will welcome a formal pledge. We know how much monthly dollars add up over years of coverage, and we know it is worth the extra effort from us. If we are right, the new AAPMA will grow very quickly, and you will soon be able to find a member in your area with a quick search on MedicarePros.org.

In the meantime, if you need a solution *now*, what should you do?

Remember the key question to ask when looking for an agent who has done the very hard and continuing work to get the licenses and maintain the annual certifications for both Medigap supplement products and for Medicare Advantage products:

"What carriers are you appointed with for Medicare Advantage, and what carriers are you appointed with for Medicare Supplements?"

We have not found a website or other resource that reliably lists brokers and independent agents representing both classes of products.

We also have not found a resource listing only Medicare Advantage independent brokers.

We have, though, found one promising resource which lists Medigap Supplement agents, at **MedicareSupp.org** The site will allow you to input your zip code, and will return a list of all member agents & brokers within a 100 mile radius, with direct contact phone numbers. At the least, that gives our readers anywhere in the country an immediate list of people who meet **half** of the requirement, so it is a starting point.

We suggest carefully screening the listed agents, as many of them are strict "Medigap Supplement Evangelists", who will not even consider selling Medicare Advantage products. As we've discussed, many agents simply do not want to invest the time, the continuing effort, and the aggravation tolerance to deal with the extra regulatory hassles required to offer Medicare Advantage. They still hold themselves out as experts, but must find a way to force-fit every client into half of the available programs.

You must find out quickly if the person you've contacted is truly an honest broker of **both** universes. So ask an additional question at the start of your conversation:

"What percentage of your business last year was Medicare Supplements and what percentage was Medicare Advantage?"

If you hear anything that indicates other than an even mix and balance, move on immediately!

It will take some work to find someone worthy of your trust and your business, so interview several people. Do not stop until you know in your heart that you have found a keeper. Your health and wellbeing for the next few decades are worth it!

We wish you great health, plenty of prosperity, and many more years to enjoy them, and we thank you for buying this book. If you've enjoyed the information, a quick review on amazon.com would be very much appreciated!

Part III

Reference

Calendar of Deadlines & Traps

Important Dates

The end of the third month after the month of your 65th birthday. Your Initial Enrollment Period (**IEP**)for Parts A and B, as well as Medicare Advantage, lasts seven months, centered on the month in which you turn 65.

Month 1	Month 2	Month 3	65	Month 5	Month 6	Month 7

The end of the sixth month after you turn 65 *and* enroll in Part B. For most of us, since we have already initiated Social Security payments, the start of Part B is automatically the 1st of the month we turn 65. If delayed, without equivalent creditable medical insurance coverage (employer-sponsored), we will be hit with Part B penalties for life.

65	Month 2	Month 3	Month 4	Month 5	Month 6

Missing this deadline means losing your **primary certain opportunity** to enroll in a Medigap supplement policy, at the lowest rates, without any medical questions or underwriting of any kind. Insurers must issue during this IEP for Medigap.

The end of one year after you first elect a Medicare Advantage plan. This is when your "**trial right**" expires, and it defines the other certain opportunity to enroll in a Medigap supplement, under Guaranteed issue rules.

December 7th of each year. This is the end of the Annual Enrollment Period (**AEP**), during which you may add, remove or change Medicare Advantage or Part D Drug Plans. AEP runs from October 15th through December 7th.

February 14th of each year. This is the end of the annual Medicare Advantage Disenrollment Period, which runs for January 1st to February 14th. During this time, you can drop a MA or MA-PD plan and return to Original Medicare.

March 31st of each year. The Part A and/or Part B Open Enrollment Period (**OEP**), during which you can sign up for Original Medicare only, if you missed your first opportunity, runs from January 1st through March 31st every year. You may have to pay penalties for periods without coverage.

Note that starting January 1st of 2019, this OEP will also contain the opportunity to disenroll from a Medicare Advantage plan **and** enroll in a new one. This is a welcome change in opening up some privileges of AEP to three more months of the year, but only allows you to **change** MA plans, not get into one for the first time. Just to keep things complicated, we guess.

June 30th of the year in which you first got Part B coverage, if you did so during OEP for that year. From April 1st to June 30th, you can sign up for a Medicare Advantage or MA-PD plan.

What can we do to fix this exploding problem?

Fixing Medicare

Proponents of Medicare For All as a fix for Obamacare as a replacement have no apparent idea of the existing complexities of the system. It would exponentially grow the nighmares of enrollment education, competent licensed advisors, time windows to avoid traps, and so on.

The current system trudges on, but it is broken, in many ways. We can't begin to cover all of them here, but we will give you an idea of the scope of the issues.

The ridiculous calendar problem

There are 57+ million members in Medicare, and they get all of **55 days** per year to add or change Medicare Advantage or prescription drug coverage in their plans. (October 15th through December 7th, the Annual Election Period, AEP)

That is more than 1 million retirees per day who need to speak to persons knowledgeable and licensed to help them.

We cannot find any reliable statistics on the

number of Medicare-licensed, or even the number of heath-licensed insurance agents in the USA. The Bureau of Labor Statistics website says there were 385,700 *total* insurance sales agents in the USA in 2018. Answers.com says there were 434,800 total in the US in2008. Total agents includes those who specialize in life insurance, the car insurance guys, the group insurance salesmen, the annuity specialists, the property & casualty people, the health specialists, and finally the Medicare-qualified health specialists.

We'll use the larger numbers for a deeper look. If a quarter of them were licensed for all Health lines, and a quarter of *them* were true Medicare experts, we are down to 27,175 to service 57 million. In 55 days. That is 2,097 members per agent, or about 38 meetings every day for almost two months.

And this does not include the 10,000 new people aging-in, turning 65, every day for the next 15 years or so. 10x the numbers of qualified agents and it still does not work. 100x -- maybe.

One more wild card: CMS prohibits Medicare Advantage agents from proactively contacting any existing or potential members by any method other than broadcast marketing, including direct mail. We may not walk up to people at health fairs or educational events. We may not knock on doors in senior communities. And heaven forbid we want to pick up the phone to actually reach out and offer help — that is a termination-level offense. People seeking help must somehow know they are in that 55 day window, somehow find our phone numbers, and call **us** during our busiest time of the year.

But this prohibition does **not** extend to agents who only sell Medigap supplements! Who made these rules?

Other than agents, there are many dedicated, well-informed volunteers who do their best to help seniors to understand the system and their options. Many of them operate under the amazing SHIPs (State Health Insurance Assistance Programs) that operate in each state. But everyone, professionals and volunteers alike, is overwhelmed by the numbers, the complexity, and the sheer volume of data. It takes a long time and a great deal of effort to learn all of the intricacies of Medicare, and then a lot of ongoing time to stay current. SHIP programs can only expect a *high* level of devotion from their volunteers, when an extraordinary level may be required.

Also — perhaps 20 to 30% of those 57 million *cannot* modify their plans in the way that would serve them best, because they want a new or different Medigap plan — and are no longer healthy enough to qualify for it.

Exclusionary Rules

Open enrollment season is limited for one major reason: insurance companies, and regulators, are historically and pathologically afraid of **adverse selection**. This is the problem that derives from the fact that people who perceive themselves to already have a significant problem will seek out financial strategies to reduce their exposure. So someone who is pretty sure they have cancer, but has yet to be officially diagnosed for some reason, will be very eager to take out a life insurance policy, because he knows it is likely to "pay off", and be a great "investment" for his family.

But this is **not** a problem of adverse selection, at least within the Medicare Advantage space. There is NO medical underwriting, ever, in MA plans. The plan carriers are actually compensated *more* by Medicare, the sicker their plan members are when entering the plan.

So why not open up the 55 day window to year-round MA open enrollment?

Adverse selection is still seen to be a huge underwriting factor in the Medigap supplement world though. Carriers do everything possible to discourage guaranteed-issue business taken outside of the Initial Enrollment Period (6 months after turning 65 and having Part B), because they would greatly prefer to do medical underwriting, and reject anyone with a hint of expensive disease. The Obamacare idea of prior continuous coverage to exclude preexisting conditions has not made it to here, so far.

If we could get that idea force-fed into the Medigap markets, it would also go a long way towards rationalizing Medicare plans.

The 5-Star Rating System

Medicare Advantage and standalone PDP plans are constantly evaluated by CMS, and each plan is given a rating annually,, on a 1-Star to 5-Star scale. This is done to maintain broad and deep oversight of plans, and also to give prospective members a shorthand method of comparing plans' effectiveness.

This system is crazy complicated. There are companies with large cadres of employees that generate a lot of revenue by just doing consulting for health insurers, to improve a plan's Star rating. The ratings are very important, in part because CMS compensates highly rated plans with **a lot** of extra money in the form of bonuses.

There are 48 categories that are rated! No doubt by literal armies of bureaucrats in acres of cube cities, funded by your tax dollars. Nobody who's talking knows how much this program costs. But just imagine the effort that goes into it. One of the many outputs of the monitoring departments is the assembly of an annual summary spreadsheet. It contains 54 columns by 635 rows of data, and every cell has a value resulting from a year of analysis. Over 34,000 summary data points that only a watching-the-watchers bureaucrat could love.

They include deep detail on such things as breast cancer screenings, colorectal cancer screenings, annual flu vaccines, improving or maintaining physical health, improving or maintaining mental health, monitoring physical activity, BMI assessments, managing chronic conditions, medication review, functional status assessments, pain assessment, osteoporosis management in women who had a fracture – on and on.

Of these 48, 14 relate directly to member feedback, so one result of the Star system is that disappointed (or delighted) members DO have a serious voice in the profit flows to their plans.

One of the primary benefits to plans awarded the full 5-Stars is that they are permitted to enroll members year-round. No 55-day window, **unlimited time to enroll**, unlimited new members. [It is noteworthy that this same benefit is accorded to plans that enroll Low Income Subsidy (LIS) and Special needs Plans (SNP) members, who tend to be much sicker that average members, the worst risks. They are apparently among the most profitable members as well, because insurers go to great lengths to attract them with spectacular benefits packages.]

So clearly, open enrollment year-round is a huge benefit to a plan, worth fighting for and paying high-end consultants.

It is also supposed to be a great benefit to members, since the whole rationale is that retirees get the very best plans at will, even during the 10+ months of the year that other plans are prohibited from taking on new members.

But not only is the rating system crazy — the results are out of bounds too. Of **635** total national MA, MA-PD, and PDP plans, only **41** are 5-Star, and only **17** of them are complete MA-PD plans. ***17 out of 630 is a meager 2.7%!*** So a prospective member's chances of finding one that's available in his or her county is less than 3%. We see the benefit to the plans' profits, but ***where is the benefit to the Medicare enrollees?***

Here is some low-hanging fruit for legislators and bureaucrats who genuinely want to improve the system: ***open up year-round enrollment for all plans achieving 4, 4.5 or 5-Stars***. Any of those is truly excellent performance. Make them available to more than 2.7% of the population! More than 50% of the people would have access to at least one plan, with this one simple change.

It would also go a long way towards ending the craziness of what has become similar to a 2 month "Open Season" on retirees among MA plan sponsors. Their mailboxes are carpet bombed every autumn. The deadlines introduce an urgency to sign up that does not have any reason to exist. Adverse Selection is clearly not a problem if the system rewards high performers with year-round open doors.

Remove the automatic hard sell of retirees by structural urgency of deadlines, replace it with relaxed ability to explore, learn about the best, and choose at will.

This would also go a long way towards rationalizing production and enrollment resources, leaving well trained employees in place year-round, instead of massive ramp-ups in insurers' headcount at the end of every summer.

And while we're at it, let's ***remove the overbearing, restrictive prohibitions on member contact*** for Medicare Advantage plans only. Coupled with rules to insure full training of all Medicare agents, below, the ability to reach out to folks aging-into the system is actually **helpful** to seniors, not something to be prohibited.

Two Universes, Biased Advisors

There are two universes of plans right now —

Medigap supplements and Medicare Advantage, and CMS seems to be doing everything it can to promote the latter, because administrators like managed care.

Retirees need unbiased, highly informed, honest brokers who know both sides of the equation, and are able to earn a living from both, to guide their decisions. It is very easy to spend 2x, 3x, even 5x as much as necessary to get adequate coverage in the Medicare add-on market, which is *absolutely essential* for adequate coverage under current law. No volunteer can be expected to know all of the intricacies, because, even for a professional who is being paid well for the effort, it is close to impossible to keep up with all of the changes.

Continuing to permit agents who are licensed for only half of the available products virtually guarantees sub-par advice for a great many retirees. How can we allow this to continue? True experts are needed. If an agent is not willing to put forth the effort to represent both, he or she should not be turned loose on seniors, and allowed to hold himself out as an expert advisor.

We can hear our phones and email blowing up right now, but that is the truth. It is about time we dealt with it.

Rationalize the licensing and certification processes across both sets of products. There is not much difference between MA HMOs and PPOs year to year, and other MA types require familiarity, only if available where the producer is licensed. Yet an agent representing more than one — which every agent should be required to do — must take annual courses for each, and pass annual tests for each. We need to fix this, because it, alone, keeps many otherwise well-intended agents from picking up MA lines. The prospect of a month or two per year, every year, devoted entirely to unpaid paperwork and repetitive certifications is quite daunting.

Fix this, by agreement of CMS and the National Association of Insurance Commissioners. Then ***require all producers to be licensed for both MA and Medigap, and appointed with at least 2 of the top 10 carriers <u>of each</u>*** *(except captive in-house sales staff)*, ***within a 2-year changeover period.***

We cannot profess to have all of the solutions to the problems of Medicare, but these few are a start. Before we stand down from the soapbox, we will take one small stab at one big fix for the healthcare system overall in the US:

Fixing US Healthcare

This topic is way beyond the scope of this book. But one obvious, gigantic problem also has one stunningly obvious fix.

The problem is the insane escalation in prescription drug prices, as each manufacturer lines up at the gravy train to load their pockets to overflowing. At the expense of all of us.

We need to develop a groundswell of support for prescription drug reform. The executives are so used to **covert collusion**, the fixing of prices by unified movement rather than by clandestine agreement, that **they cannot even see themselves for what they have become: modern day gangsters, profiting off of a human need even greater than opioid addiction — the need for life itself.**

They have brought this upon themselves. We now seem to have a whole industry of closet Martin Shkrelis, pushing prices up as much as the market (especially Medicare, **prohibited** from negotiating drug prices by a legion of lobbyists and corrupt politicians!) will bear. Recall that Shkreli is the convicted felon CEO who in 2015 raised the price of a 62 year old drug used to treat a life-threatening infectious disease from $13.50 per pill to $750.00 per pill, overnight. That is an instant 5,500% increase, simply because he had the power to do it, without being charged with murder for those his greed killed.

This is not an uncommon event. Numerous executives have increased the prices of many dozens of drugs from hundreds of percent, to thousands-of-percent, simply because they could.

There is no need for back-room ACTUAL illegal price collusion, when conferences, symposiums, and even trial balloon press releases broadcast every company's intent to go to yet more ridiculous price levels — always in the name of R&D and surviving insanely long timelines for FDA approval of new drugs.

But this industry is perhaps the single **most** politically protected class, diffuse and hard to assign direct blame that threatens profits, companies or jail time. Shkreli is no cautionary example, for he simply went off the chain in every possible arrogant way, and waved it in everyone's face. It is very easy for established managers to avoid his fate of 7 years in prison.

WE PROPOSE a broad societal move towards considering Pharmas to be like private utilities.

We would never tolerate an electric company boosting rates from $100 per month year round, to $2000 per month in December through February, because people would die from electric bill poverty, freezing to death. It would be seen as criminal behavior, and the executives would be arrested, if the people didn't hang them first.

Electric companies became regulated a century ago because the necessity for their grids and the obvious waste of duplicating them created natural monopolies for an essential service, and therefore unlimited pricing power. The people did not tolerate the use of that power to create a "your money, or your life" threat.

Artificially exorbitant pricing of prescription drugs is no different. People need them for their very survival. They are not an optional purchase. And the research and approval process for new drugs, abetted by the easy extension of patents with nothing truly "new", has created long lasting monopolies or duopolies within many classes of essential drugs. Allowing the gangsters among the drug makers to exercise that systemic exclusivity to steal as much money as possible from all of us – must be stopped.

Utilities are guaranteed a modest profit, with rates set by commissions of experts. We submit that we need a major move towards that model, perhaps the **creation of a Federal Pharmaceutical**

Commission, charged with calculating and enforcing rational prices in every possible case, collapsing overhead fluff, and ensuring reasonable, consistent profits. Shrink the C-suites and the jets and the marketing profligacy, fully fund R&D.

Especially, shrink marketing profligacy. Why does nearly every drug that bombards us with ongoing, direct-to-consumer TV blitzes charge a preposterous $500 to $1,000 per month for less than an ounce of product? So that they can easily afford to bombard us with those same ads, forever!

It is only possible because we let them. Because this is America, and we Do Not Dictate Profits. Because they return a portion of those outsized profits (small by percentage, but enormous in dollar size) to the campaign coffers of the politicians in charge of regulating them, and a large portion to the expensive lobbyists with the connections to assure the politicians' action.

They have now brought an unprecedented level of regulation upon themselves, by their limitless, unprecedented greed. It cannot be allowed to continue, regardless of political uproar.

Outlaw all direct-to-consumer prescription pharmaceutical ads. After all, the whole idea of a prescription is that it needs to be the doctor who decides the remedy, not the untrained consumer. **Advertise only to doctors**, and give them the power to make decisions without popular pressure from patients who identify with a charismatic actor, appearing on their big screens several times a day.

This is the law of the land in every country other than ours, save for one. And the lack of any real attempt to control price increases is driving an enormous portion of our overall healthcare cost explosion. Our legislators are completely blinded to this simple first step by the piles of money laid in front of their eyes, year after year, by the pharmaceutical industry. Why is this step never spoken of by anyone purporting to try for real progress in reducing the ridiculous prices of drugs?

It is because this is a very heavy lift. It will take an extraordinary leader to make such a thing happen. Someone who is not afraid of political backlash the likes of which has rarely been seen. Coming from all quarters, backed by completely unlimited funding in the pursuit of a continued license to steal. Someone who is willing to take the heat, in the certain knowledge that the wellbeing of the American people <u>requires</u> it. Without a complete overhaul, can we imagine how bad the situation will be 10 years hence?

It will take someone acting <u>not</u> out of a desire to achieve a single-payer health system, not driven by the predictable ideologies of the left-wing social progressives, whose true motivator is permanent political power. It will take someone whom the people know loathes the fact that such an action has become necessary.

When such a person stands up, we should each go an extra mile to support him, and any politicians who "get it" and unite with him, when the automatic-opposition flies into a fury. It would be a political battle like few ever seen before.

States with Under-65 Medigap laws

According to a report by the Kaiser Family Foundation, there are 30 states that require insurers to offer at least one Medigap plan to qualifying Medicare beneficiaries under 65. Certain states guarantee coverage options for those with End Stage Renal Disease, for those with a disability, or both.

These state requirements can have a big impact on Medigap applicants under 65. For example, if you live in California and have Medicare coverage due to ESRD, a Medigap insurance company is not legally required to offer you a Medigap plan. The state only protects applicants under 65 with a qualifying disability.

The following chart details the states that legally require Medigap plans to those under 65, along with the health requirements to qualify.

State	Disabled Beneficiaries	Beneficiaries with ESRD
California	✓	
Colorado	✓	✓
Connecticut	✓	✓
Delaware		✓
Florida	✓	✓
Georgia	✓	✓
Hawaii	✓	✓
Illinois	✓	✓
Kansas	✓	✓
Louisiana	✓	✓
Maine	✓	✓
Maryland	✓	✓
Massachusetts	✓	
Michigan	✓	✓
Minnesota	✓	✓
Mississippi	✓	✓
Missouri	✓	✓
New Hampshire	✓	✓
New Jersey	✓	✓
New Mexico	✓	✓
New York	✓	✓
North Carolina	✓	✓
Oklahoma	✓	✓
Oregon	✓	✓
Pennsylvania	✓	✓
South Dakota	✓	✓
Tennessee	✓	✓
Texas	✓	✓
Vermont	✓	
Wisconsin	✓	✓

State-level Extra Help Programs

State Pharmaceutical Assistance Programs (SPAPs)

The following info is taken from the National Conference of State Legislators, who do a good job trying to keep up with constantly changing state-level programs:

Updated 2014; material added January 2016

Prescription drug assistance has been a substantial and growing state interest for a number of years, generally in response to residents who lack insurance coverage for medicines or who were not eligible for other government programs. In fact, the first states to authorize and fund direct subsidy programs did so in 1975. Between 2000 and 2006 at least 26 states authorized and/or started pharmaceutical assistance programs, many intended to aid low-income elderly or persons with disabilities who do not qualify for Medicaid. By 2009, a total of at least 42 states had established or authorized some type of program to provide pharmaceutical coverage or assistance; several of those are not currently operational. The subsidy programs, often termed "SPAPs," utilize state funds to pay for a portion of the costs, usually for a defined population that meets enrollment criteria. In addition, an increasing number of states use discounts or bulk purchasing approaches that do not spend state funds for the drug purchases, listed as "Discount Programs" below. Since the passage of the federal Affordable Care Act (ACA), state legislatures have been less active on SPAP issues.

CHANGING NUMBERS AND FEATURES:

38 states enacted laws over the past 30 years to create SPAP programs; others were created by executive branch action only.

For 2015-16, 22 states had 40 state subsidy programs certified by CMS/HHS as supplementing Medicare or as "SPAPs" as for the purpose of determining whether the state-administerd programs were exempt or excluded from calculations of "Medicaid Best Price." This calculation does not constitute federal regulation of these SPAPs.

22 operational programs provide for a direct subsidy using state funds; in the past five years a high point of 36 states' laws (plus DC) authorized such subsidies. Iowa has a temporary program that may close when funds are exhausted.

27 states created or authorized programs that offer a discount only (no subsidy) for eligible or enrolled residents; of these about 16 are in operation. The latest are in Florida and Iowa, starting in 2008. Some of these states also have a separate subsidy program.

Several programs ceased operation: North Carolina ended its subsidy program in 2011; South Carolina closed its subsidy program in 2010; Arizona closed its subsidy program 2009. Five others closed in January 2006, replaced by Medicare Part D plans. These include Florida, Kansas, Michigan, Minnesota and North Carolina, plus discount plans in Arkansas and South Carolina. Recent but no-longer-operational programs are listed below., with details in an offline NCSL Rx Archive Appendix for comparative and historical reference.

The most recent map of coverage available is dated in 2011:

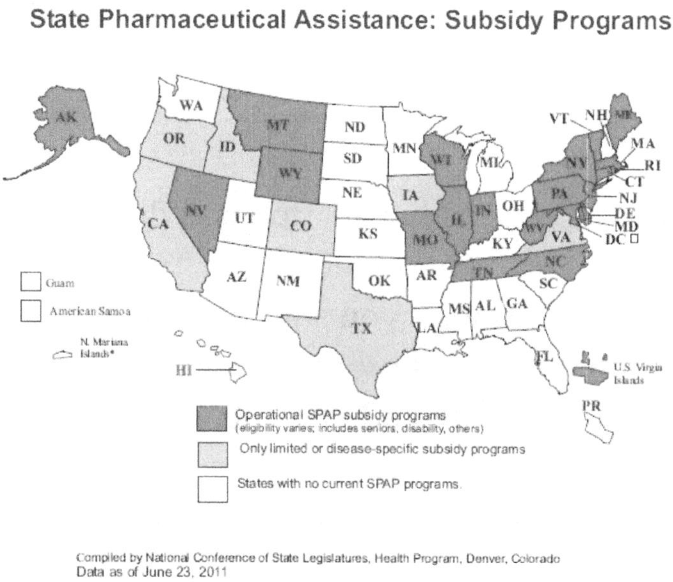

For much more detail, including state-by-state breakdowns of past an present programs, visit:

http://www.ncsl.org/research/health/state-pharmaceutical-assistance-programs.aspx

Recommended Resources for Additional Information

Medicare.gov

A deep and useful resource for most Medicare questions, particularly useful for finding and comparing coverages of Medicare Advantage plans and Prescription Drug Plans.

Includes a reasonably well updated database of providers for each plan under the tab "Sign Up/Change Plans", though you should always check directly with a listed provider before being certain that he or she is included in a particular network. CMS is cracking down on insurers for giving them out of date data on their network providers, which is then posted into this database.

Sign Up/Change Plans is also an excellent resource for entering specific prescription drugs to determine formulary tiering across multiple plans. It will allow you to input your drug and dosage list, and remember it for future sessions. **Tip**: Be sure to write down the identifier number given, for future searches.

It has less reliable but still useful estimates of

annual out of pocket costs in competing PDPs, with your exact drug list in your location with your local pharmacies.

When it comes to Medigap plans, the site is much less useful. The information does not appear on the main Sign Up tab, but under the 5th tab, "Supplements & Other Insurance". It seems like this info has been ignored, which could be on purpose, as CMS seems to be increasingly pushing people towards Medicare Advantage managed care. The info on specific plans available by zip code is often wrong, showing no plans available when there are in fact dozens. And when data does display, it often shows absurdly high annual cost estimates for Plans A through N, when in fact the annual costs are limited to the premium (for Plan F) plus drug costs (largely taken care of with a simple add-on PDP).

For general information regarding coverage items, be aware that with statements that a Part of Medicare "covers" an item, this is always subject to deductibles, co-pays, and coinsurance, which can be complex and very substantial. This creates false impressions of low to no out of pocket costs.

Navigating this site can be challenging.

Medicare Appeals booklet

https://www.medicare.gov/Pubs/pdf/11525.pdf

The Medicare Rights Center

A national, nonprofit consumer service organization that works to ensure access to affordable health care for older adults and people with disabilities through counseling and advocacy, educational programs, and public policy initiatives.

www.medicarerights.org

MedicarePros.org

Website of the new American Association of Professional Medicare Advisors, an organization dedicated to the provision of impartial, highly knowledgeable advice and guidance for seniors in need of Medicare add-on products.

It includes a lookup feature to help users find and contact pre-screened, dedicated independent health insurance agents and brokers in their area. A requirement for membership is that each agent or broker must be currently certified and active with several carriers form each of the two universes of Medicare add-on products, Medicare Advantage (Part C), and Medicare Supplements (Medigap).

National Council on Aging

Among other great resources, NCOA has an excellent benefits finder engine, to help you locate specific programs in your area, with your income level, etc.

https://www.benefitscheckup.org/

Q1medicare.com

For all the details and intricate calculations of what happens with Low Income Subsidy (**LIS**) qualifying participants in the Part D Donut Hole, the most comprehensive explanation we have found is here:

https://q1medicare.com/PartD-The-2018-Medicare-Part-D-Outlook.php

Q1medicare.com is an excellent, reliable Medicare resource.

The Center for Medicare Advocacy

A national, nonprofit, non-partisan law organization that works to advance access to comprehensive Medicare coverage and quality health care for older people and people with disabilities through legal analysis, education, and advocacy.

www.medicareadvocacy.org

SHIP State Program Locator

https://www.shiptacenter.org/

NextMountainAdvisors.com

Our site, where we will publish ongoing updates to this book, to keep our readers abreast of the many inevitable changes to Medicare and Medicaid. We will also update changes to private insurance plan rules, such as Medicare Advantage and Medigap supplements.

Readers of this book may use the site to ask specific questions, and we will try to answer every one.

Glossary

Accreditation

A process where external organizations (or "accrediting bodies") evaluate health care facilities' policies, procedures, and performance to make sure they are meeting predetermined criteria.

ADL

Activities of Daily Living, routine activities that people tend do every day without needing assistance. There are six basic ADLs: eating, bathing, dressing, toileting, transferring (walking) and continence. The performance of these ADLs is important for determining what type of long-term care – for example. nursing-home care or in-home care – and health coverage such as Medicare, Medicaid or long-term care insurance a person will need as they grow older. Needing assistance with two or more is typically needed before benefits from a Long Term Care (LTC) insurance policy will kick in.

Advance Beneficiary Notice of Noncoverage (ABN)

In Original Medicare, a notice that a doctor, supplier, or provider gives a person with Medicare before furnishing an item or service if the doctor, supplier, or provider believes that Medicare may deny payment. In this situation, if you aren't given an ABN before you get the item or service, and Medicare denies payment, then you may not have to pay for it. If you are given an ABN, and you sign it, you'll probably have to pay for the item or service if Medicare denies payment.

Advance coverage decision

A notice you get from a Medicare Advantage Plan letting you know in advance whether it will cover a particular service.

Advance directive

A written document stating how you want medical decisions to be made if you lose the ability to make them for yourself. It may include a living will and a durable power of attorney for health care.

Adverse Selection

In the insurance industry overall, risk is mitigated by having a broad pool of policyholders who represent the "average" risks of the targeted populations. This makes it possible for their actuaries, a group of highly educated and extremely talented mathematicians, to develop models of expected loss ratios based on deep statistical databases — and therefore for the insurance company to sell policies with rates appropriate for all expected risks, overhead and costs, plus a predictable operating profit.

Life insurers would fail quickly if, for example, people were able to buy standard rated policies upon receiving a diagnosis of Stage IV cancer. This is an extreme example of adverse selection. Insurance cannot become an open casino window for paying in small a few times, and collecting big quickly on a known event.

Procedures and underwriting standards are therefore put in place to limit or eliminate the risks of people gaming the system when they have reason to know that their possibility of a large payout is much greater than the insurer's rates would indicate.

ALF

Assisted Living Facility

ALJ

A hearing before an Administrative law Judge is usually the fourth step of escalation in the Medicare appeals process

ALS

Amyotrophic lateral sclerosis, also known as Lou Gehrig's disease.

Ambulatory surgical center

A facility where certain surgeries may be performed for patients who aren't expected to need more than 24 hours of care.

Angina pectoris

Chest pain.

Angioplasty

A medical procedure used to open a blocked artery.

Annual Election Period (AEP)

The time from October 15th to December 7th of each year when Medicare enrollees are permitted to enter, or switch between, Medicare Advantage, MA-PD, and Prescription Drug Plans. Also referred to as open enrollment.

Appeal

See also **Grievance**, below. An appeal is the action you can take if you disagree with a coverage or payment decision made by Medicare, your Medicare health plan, or your Medicare Prescription Drug Plan. You can appeal if Medicare or your plan denies one of these:

- Your request for a health care service, supply, item, or prescription drug that you think you should be able to get
- Your request for payment for a health care service, supply, item, or prescription drug you already got
- Your request to change the amount you must pay for a health care service, supply, item or

prescription drug.

You can also appeal if Medicare or your plan stops providing or paying for all or part of a service, supply, item, or prescription drug you think you still need.

Assignment

An agreement by your doctor, provider, or supplier to be paid directly by Medicare, to accept the payment amount Medicare approves for the service (Medicare-approved Amount, or MAA), and not to bill you for any more than the Medicare deductible and coinsurance. It is illegal for a doctor on an assignment contract to bill you for Excess Charges.

Attained Age

One of three available rating classes for pricing of Medigap policies. The participant's age at each policy anniversary determines the rate for the policy, except that increases for reasons other than aging additional years are permitted. The other two classes are Issue Age and Community Rated.

Beneficiary

A person who has health care insurance through the Medicare or Medicaid programs.

Beneficiary and Family Centered Care Quality Improvement Organization (BFCC-QIO)

A type of QIO (an organization of doctors and other health care experts under contract with Medicare) that uses doctors and other health care experts to review complaints and quality of care for people with Medicare. The BFCC-QIO makes sure there is consistency in the case review process while taking into consideration local factors and local needs, including general quality of care and medical necessity.

Benefit period

The way that Original Medicare measures your use of hospital and skilled nursing facility (SNF) services. A benefit period begins the day you're admitted as an inpatient in a hospital or SNF. The benefit period ends when you haven't gotten any inpatient hospital care (or skilled care in a SNF) for 60 days in a row. If you go into a hospital or a SNF after one benefit period has ended, a new benefit period begins. You must pay the inpatient hospital deductible for each benefit period. There's no limit to the number of benefit periods.

Benefits

The health care items or services covered under a health insurance plan. Covered benefits and excluded services are defined in the health insurance plan's coverage documents.

Benefits Coordination & Recovery Center

The company that acts on behalf of Medicare to collect and manage information on other types of insurance or coverage that a person with Medicare may have, and determine whether the coverage pays before or after Medicare. This company also acts on behalf of Medicare to obtain repayment when Medicare makes a conditional payment, and the other payer is determined to be primary.

Centers for Medicare & Medicaid Services (CMS)

The federal agency that runs the Medicare, Medicaid, and Children's Health Insurance Programs, and the federally facilitated Marketplace.

CHAMPVA

A health care benefit for dependents of qualifying veterans.

Chargemaster

A hospital's secret internal maximum (ridiculous) price list of every procedure, every pill, every service. Always insanely overpriced relative to what they ever expect to collect from insurance companies, and completely unrelated to actual cost.

Items can be priced at as much a 400 **times** cost, which would be a 20,000% retail markup. These charges are presented with a straight face to the uninsured and the near-poor, and pursued relentlessly by collections agents. Medicare will only pay, on average, about 8% to 11% of these numbers.

Children's Health Insurance Program (CHIP)

Insurance program jointly funded by state and federal government that provides health coverage to low-income children and, in some states, pregnant women in families who earn too much income to qualify for Medicaid but can't afford to purchase private health insurance coverage.

Claim

A request for payment that you submit to Medicare or other health insurance when you get items and services that you think are covered.

Clinical breast exam

An exam by your doctor or other health care provider to check for breast cancer by feeling and looking at your breasts. This exam isn't the same as a mammogram and is usually done in the doctor's office during your Pap test and pelvic exam.

Coinsurance

An amount you may be required to pay as your share of the cost for services after you pay any deductibles. Coinsurance is usually a percentage (for example, 20%).

Community Rated

One of three available rating classes for pricing of Medigap policies. The participant's age at each policy anniversary determines the rate for the policy, but pricing must be consistent with all other members of the same age within the same state or other large region, regardless of gender. The other two classes are Issue Age and Attained Age.

Comprehensive outpatient rehabilitation facility

A facility that provides a variety of services on an outpatient basis, including physicians' services, physical therapy, social or psychological services, and rehabilitation.

Coordination of benefits

A way to figure out who pays first when 2 or more health insurance plans are responsible for paying the same medical claim.

Co-payment (Co-pay)

An amount you may be required to pay as your share of the cost for a medical service or supply, like a doctor's visit, hospital outpatient visit, or prescription drug. A copayment is usually a set amount, rather than a percentage. For example, you might pay $10 or $20 for a doctor's visit or prescription drug.

Coronary stent

A device used to keep an artery open.

Cost sharing

An amount you may be required to pay as your share of the cost for a medical service or supply, like a doctor's visit, hospital outpatient visit, or prescription drug. This amount can include copayments, coinsurance, and/or deductibles.

Coverage determination (Part D)

The first decision made by your Medicare drug plan (not the pharmacy) about your drug benefits, including:

- Whether a particular drug is covered
- Whether you have met all the requirements for getting a requested drug
- How much you're required to pay for a

drug

- Whether to make an exception to a plan rule when you request it

The drug plan must give you a prompt decision (72 hours for standard requests, 24 hours for expedited requests). If you disagree with the plan's coverage determination, the next step is an appeal.

Coverage gap (Medicare prescription drug coverage)

A period of time in which you pay higher cost sharing for prescription drugs until you spend enough to qualify for catastrophic coverage. The coverage gap (also called the "**donut hole**") starts when you and your plan have paid a set dollar amount for prescription drugs during that year. For 2018, the gap starts at $3,750 and ends at $5,000. See extensive discussion in Chapter 4.

Creditable coverage

Previous health insurance coverage that can be used to shorten a pre-existing condition waiting period under a Medigap policy.

Creditable prescription drug coverage

Prescription drug coverage (for example, from an employer or union) that's expected to pay, on average, at least as much as Medicare's standard prescription drug coverage. People who have this kind of coverage when they become eligible for Medicare can generally keep that coverage without paying a penalty, if they decide to enroll in Medicare prescription drug coverage later.

Critical access hospital (CAH)

A small facility that provides outpatient services, as well as inpatient services on a limited basis, to people in rural areas.

C-SNP

Chronic disease Special Needs Plan, a type fo Medicare Advantage plan for people with chronic health problems.

Custodial care

Non-skilled personal care, like help with activities of daily living like bathing, dressing, eating, getting in or out of a bed or chair, moving around, and using the bathroom. It may also include the kind of health-related care that most people do themselves, like using eye drops. In most cases, Medicare doesn't pay for custodial care.

Deductible

The amount you must pay for health care or prescriptions before Original Medicare, your prescription drug plan, or your other insurance begins to pay.

Deemed status

A provider or supplier earns this when they have been accredited by a national accreditation program (approved by the Centers for Medicare & Medicaid Services) that they demonstrate compliance with certain conditions.

Demonstrations

Special projects, sometimes called "pilot programs" or "research studies," that test improvements in Medicare coverage, payment, and quality of care. They usually operate only for a limited time, for a specific group of people, and in specific areas.

Dental coverage

Benefits that help pay for the cost of visits to a dentist for basic or preventive services, like teeth cleaning, X-rays, and fillings.

Department of Health and Human Services (HHS; DHS previously)

The federal agency that oversees CMS, which administers programs for protecting the health of all Americans, including Medicare, the Marketplace, Medicaid, and the Children's Health Insurance Program (CHIP).

Diagnostic mammogram

An X-ray exam of the breast in a woman who either has a breast problem or has had a change show up on a screening mammogram.

DME Medicare Administrative Contractor (MAC)

A private company that contracts with Medicare to pay bills for durable medical equipment.

Donut Hole

See Coverage Gap, above, and Chapter 4.

Drug list (Formulary)

A list of prescription drugs covered by a prescription drug plan or another insurance plan offering prescription drug benefits. This list is also called a formulary.

D-SNP

Dual-eligible Special Needs Plan, a type of Medicare Advantage plan for Dual Eligibles, next:

Dual Eligible Medicare beneficiary

A person who is enrolled in both Medicare and Medicaid, by virtue of very low income and assets. The limits for 2018, in general, are $1,032/month in income if single, and $2,000 in available assets. Married couples face tougher qualifying, with a combined income limit of $1,391/

month and $3,000 in assets. Certain exceptions, especially for home equity, mmedical costs and old bills, may apply. Check with your local office of the state department of social services or its equivalent to see if you can qualify.

Dual Eligibles are able to get zero premium Medicare Advantage plans that have deductibles, co-pays and coinsurance reduced to near-zero as well. It is the closest thing to a congressional health plan that you can get, without being elected to congress!

Durable medical equipment (DME)

Certain medical equipment, like a walker, wheelchair, or hospital bed, that's ordered by your doctor for use in the home.

Durable power of attorney

A legal document that names someone else to make health care decisions for you. This is helpful if you become unable to make your own decisions.

Employer or union retiree plans

Plans that give health and/or drug coverage to employees, former employees, and their families. These plans are offered to people through their (or a spouse's) current or former employer or employee organization.

End-Stage Renal Disease (ESRD)

Permanent kidney failure that requires a regular course of dialysis or a kidney transplant.

Exception

A type of Medicare prescription drug coverage determination. A formulary exception is a drug plan's decision to cover a drug that's not on its drug list or to waive a coverage rule. A tiering exception is a drug plan's decision to charge a lower amount for a drug that's on its non-preferred drug tier. You or your prescriber must request an exception, and your doctor or other prescriber must provide a supporting statement explaining the medical reason for the exception.

Excess charge

If you have Original Medicare, and the amount a doctor or other health care provider is legally permitted to charge is higher than the Medicare-approved amount, the difference is called the excess charge. It is limited to 15% of the MAA, and it cannot be charged to you if the doctor has agreed to accept Assignment, above.

Extra Help

A Medicare program to help people with limited income and resources pay Medicare prescription drug program costs, like premiums, deductibles, and coinsurance. See Low Income Subsidy (**LIS**), and Chapter 7.

Federally qualified health center

Federally funded nonprofit health centers or clinics that serve medically underserved areas and populations. Federally qualified health centers provide primary care services even if you can't afford it. Services are provided on a sliding scale fee based on your ability to pay.

Five Star (5-Star) Rated Plan

A Medicare Advantage or MAPD plan receiving the ephemeral 5-Star rating from CMS, which gives it the special right to enroll new members year-round instead of just October 15th to December 7th (the Annual Election Period, or open enrollment).

In reality, only a small percentage of retirees will have access to such a plan. Of 630 total national MA, MA-PD, and PDP plans, only 41 are 5-Star, and only 17 of them are complete plans. 17 out of 630 is a meager 2.7%. So your chances of finding one that's available in your county is less than 3%.

Formulary

A list of prescription drugs covered by a prescription drug plan or another insurance plan offering prescription drug benefits. Also called a drug list.

FPL

Federal Poverty Level, currently set at $1,005 per month for a single individual and $1,353 for a married couple, is the dividing line or basis for many income-based benefit programs.

Generic drug

A prescription drug that has the same active-ingredient formula as a brand-name drug. Generic drugs usually cost less than brand-name drugs. The Food and Drug Administration (FDA) rates these drugs to be as safe and effective as brand-name drugs.

Grievance

Technically, this is a complaint about the way your Medicare health plan or Medicare drug plan is giving care. For example, you may file a grievance if you have a problem calling the plan or if you're unhappy with the way a staff person at the plan has behaved towards you. However, if you have a complaint about a plan's refusal to cover a service, supply, or prescription, you file an appeal.

However, this is the **power term** to use when speaking to your private insurer customer service center about **any problem or coverage decision**, as you simultaneously request escalation of your call to a Supervisor.

This term gets their attention quickly, as it implies that your matter is about to be referred directly to CMS, making management not only aware of the issue, but forced to respond quickly to a summons from a higher authority. Which is of course the last thing they want.

Invoking this term triggers the dislike of bureaucracy in the people you need to grant you a favorable decision. You turn the tables, because they now face the wall of process and procedure just like you, at an even higher stress level.

Your complaint may be more properly handled by a **Appeal**, above, but that term fails to produce the emotional reaction in the customer service staff that may lead to an immediate reversal.

Group health plan

In general, a health plan offered by an employer or employee organization that provides health coverage to employees and their families.

Guaranteed issue rights (also called "Medigap protections")

Rights you have in certain situations when insurance companies are required by law to sell or offer you a Medigap policy. In these situations, an insurance company can't deny you a Medigap policy, or place conditions on a Medigap policy, like exclusions for pre-existing conditions, and can't charge you more for a Medigap policy because of a past or present health problem. See details in Chapter 5.

Guaranteed renewable policy

An insurance policy that can't be terminated by the insurance company unless you make untrue statements to the insurance company, commit fraud, or don't pay your premiums. All Medigap policies issued since 1992 are guaranteed renewable. Premiums are permitted to increase as necessary, monitored by state insurance commissioners.

Health care provider

A person or organization that's licensed to give health care. Doctors, nurses, and hospitals are examples of health care providers.

Health coverage

Legal entitlement to payment or reimbursement for your health care costs, generally under a contract with a health insurance company, a group health plan offered in connection with employment, or a government program like Medicare, Medicaid, or the Children's Health Insurance Program (CHIP).

Health Insurance Marketplace

A service that helps people shop for and enroll in affordable health insurance. The federal government operates the Marketplace, available at **HealthCare.gov,** for most states. Some states run their own Marketplaces.

The Health Insurance Marketplace (also known as the "Marketplace" or "exchange") provides health plan shopping and enrollment services through websites, call centers, and in-person help.

Health Insurance Portability and Accountability Act of 1996 (HIPAA)

The "Standard for Privacy of Individually Identifiable Health Information (also called the "Privacy Rule")" of HIPAA assures your health information is properly protected while allowing the flow of health information needed to provide and promote high quality health care and to protect the public's health and well being.

High-deductible Medigap policy

A type of Medigap policy that has a high deductible but a lower premium. You must pay the deductible before the Medigap policy pays anything. The deductible amount can change.

Homebound

To be homebound means:

- You have trouble leaving your home without help (like using a cane, wheelchair, walker, or crutches; special transportation; or help from another person) because of an illness or injury, or

- Leaving your home isn't recommended because of your condition, and you're normally unable to leave your home because it's a major effort

You may leave home for medical treatment or short, infrequent absences for non-medical reasons, like attending religious services. You can still get home health care if you attend adult day care.

Home health agency

An organization that provides in-home health care.

Home health care (HHC)

Health care services and supplies a doctor decides you may get in your home under a plan of care established by your doctor. Medicare only covers home health care on a limited basis as ordered by your doctor.

Hospice

A special way of caring for people who are terminally ill. Hospice care involves a team-oriented approach that addresses the medical, physical, social, emotional, and spiritual needs of the patient. Hospice also provides support to the patient's family or caregiver.

Hospital outpatient setting

A part of a hospital where you get outpatient services, like an emergency department, observation unit, surgery center, or pain clinic.

Hospital-related medical condition

Any condition that was treated during your qualifying 3-day inpatient hospital stay, even if it wasn't the reason you were admitted to the hospital.

Household Discount

A premium discount available on most Medigap supplement policies when domestic partners get their plans from the same company. It is usually in the 4% to 7% range, and applies to both policies.

Independent reviewer

An organization (sometimes called an Independent Review Entity or IRE) that has no connection to your Medicare health plan or Medicare Prescription Drug Plan. Medicare contracts with the IRE to review your case if you appeal your plan's payment or coverage decision or if your plan doesn't make a timely appeals decision.

Initial Coverage Phase (ICP)

Once you've met your yearly Part D deductible, you'll pay a co-payment or coinsurance for each covered drug until you reach your plan's

Initial Coverage Limit, which is $3,750 in 2018. You'll then enter your plan's coverage gap (also called the "donut hole"). See lengthy discussion in Chapter 4.

Initial Election Period (IEP)

Your first opportunity to take Parts A and B, as well as a Medicare Advantage or Medigap supplement plan. See Calendar of Deadlines.

In-network

Doctors, hospitals, pharmacies, and other health care providers that have agreed to provide members of a certain insurance plan with services and supplies at a discounted price. In some insurance plans, your care is only covered if you get it from in-network doctors, hospitals, pharmacies, and other health care providers.

Inpatient care

Health care that you get when you're admitted to a health care facility, like a hospital or skilled nursing facility.

Inpatient hospital care

Treatment you get in an acute care hospital, critical access hospital, inpatient rehabilitation facility, long-term care hospital, inpatient care as part of a qualifying research study, and mental health care.

Inpatient hospital services

Services you get when you're admitted to a hospital, including bed and board, nursing services, diagnostic or therapeutic services, and medical or surgical services.

Inpatient prospective payment system (IPPS)

Hospitals that have contracted with Medicare to provide acute inpatient care and accept a predetermined rate as payment in full.

Inpatient rehabilitation facility

A hospital, or part of a hospital, that provides an intensive rehabilitation program to inpatients.

IRE

An Independent Review Entity is an separate organization with which Medicare contracts to handle the second level of appeals of a denial of coverage (except for of hospital care) if you are in a Medicare Advantage Plan or Medicare private drug plan (Part D).

IRMAA

You'll get a notice if you have Medicare Part B and/or Part D, and Social Security determines that any Income Related Monthly Adjustment Amounts (IRMAA) apply to you. The higher your income, the more it will cost you. This notice includes information about Social Security's determination and appeal rights.

I-SNP

Institutional Special Needs Plan. Institutional Special Needs plans restrict enrollment to Medicare Advantage eligible individuals who, for 90 days or longer, require or are expected to need the level of services provided in a long-term care (LTC) skilled nursing facility (SNF), a LTC nursing facility (NF), a SNF/NF, an intermediate care facility (ICF) for the developmentally disabled, an inpatient psychiatric facility, or an assisted living facility (ALF).

Issue Age

One of three available rating classes for pricing of Medigap policies. The participant's age when the policy is first issued determines the rate for the life of the policy, except that increases for reasons other than aging additional years are permitted. The other two classes are Attained Age and Community Rated.

Large group health plan

In general, a group health plan that covers employees of either an employer or employee organization that has at least 100 employees.

Lifetime reserve days

In Original Medicare, these are additional days that Medicare will pay for when you're in a hospital for more than 90 days. You have a total of 60 reserve days that can be used during your lifetime. For each lifetime reserve day, Medicare pays all covered costs except for a daily coinsurance – but that amount is currently $670 per day.

Limiting charge

In Original Medicare, the highest amount of money you can be charged for a covered service by doctors and other health care suppliers who don't accept assignment. The limiting charge is 15% over Medicare's approved amount. The limiting charge only applies to certain services and doesn't apply to supplies or equipment.

Living will

A written legal document, also called a "medical directive" or "advance directive." It shows what type of treatments you want or don't want in case you can't speak for yourself, like whether you want life support. Usually, this document only comes into effect if you're unconscious.

Long-term care (LTC)

Services that include medical and non-medical care provided to people who are unable to perform basic activities of daily living, like dressing or bathing. Long-term supports and services can be provided at home, in the community, in assisted living, or in nursing homes. Individuals may need long-term supports and services at any age. Medicare and most health insurance plans don't pay for long-term care.

Long-term care hospital

Acute care hospitals that provide treatment for patients who stay, on average, more than 25 days. Most patients are transferred from an intensive or critical care unit. Services provided include comprehensive rehabilitation, respiratory therapy, head trauma treatment, and pain management.

Long-term Care Ombudsman

An independent advocate (supporter) for nursing home and assisted living facility residents who works to solve problems of residents of nursing homes, assisted living facilities, or similar facilities. They may be able to provide information about home health agencies in their area.

Loss Ratio

The portion of collected premiums that a plan consumes directly paying benefits for members. Subject to regulatory minimums set by state and federal authorities when applying for rate changes.

Low Income Subsidy (LIS)

Also called "**Extra Help**", this is a federal program that helps with Part D prescription drug plan premiums, deductibles, and co-pays for those with qualifying low income. See Chapter 7.

MAA

Medicare-Approved Amount. See below.

MAC

Medicare Administrative Contractor, below.

MA Trial Right

A one-time, one year long right given to new Medicare Advantage enrollees, to revert to Original Medicare and elect to join or re-join a Medigap supplement plan without medical questions or exams, height/weight restrictions, or medication checklists.

Medicaid

A joint federal and state program that helps with medical costs for some people with limited income and resources. Medicaid programs vary from state to state, but most health care costs are covered if you qualify for both Medicare and Medicaid.

Medicaid has income and assets limitations that vary by state, but typically fall around 100% of the Federal Poverty Line on income, as updated by the US Dept. of Health and Human Services annually

Medicaid-certified provider

A health care provider (like a home health agency, hospital, nursing home, or dialysis facility) that's been approved by Medicaid. Providers are approved or "certified" if they've passed an inspection conducted by a state government agency.

Medicaid office

A state or local agency that can give information about, and help with applications for, Medicaid programs that help pay medical bills for people with limited income and resources.

Medicaid Spend-down

The process of deliberately depleting one's assets and income in order to qualify for Medicaid. For families who have not been able to afford the high cost of Long Term Care insurance, this is the only way to get care for a loved one requiring nursing home care, because Medicare does not cover it. The nursing home benefit in Medicare covers only short term stays following a hospitalization, not longer term custodial care. Spend-down typically reduces savings to a very low level, endangering the lifestyle, or even the survivability, of the remaining spouse, especially of a senior with Alzheimer's or other disease of slow death.

Medical emergency

When you believe you have an injury or illness that requires immediate medical attention to prevent a disability or death.

Medically necessary

Health care services or supplies needed to diagnose or treat an illness, injury, condition, disease, or its symptoms and that meet accepted standards of medicine.

Medical underwriting

The process that an insurance company uses to decide, based on your medical history, whether to take your application for insurance, whether to add a waiting period for pre-existing conditions (if your state law allows it), and how much to charge you for that insurance.

Medicare

Medicare is the federal health insurance program for people who are 65 or older, certain younger people with disabilities, and people with End-Stage Renal Disease (permanent kidney failure requiring dialysis or a transplant, sometimes called ESRD).

Medicare Administrative Contractor

(MAC)

A company that processes claims for Medicare.

Medicare Advantage Plan (Part C)

A type of Medicare health plan offered by a private company that contracts with Medicare to provide you with all of your Part A and Part B benefits. Medicare Advantage Plans include Health Maintenance Organizations, Preferred Provider Organizations, Private Fee-for-Service Plans, Special Needs Plans, and Medicare Medical Savings Account Plans. If you're enrolled in a Medicare Advantage Plan, most Medicare services are covered through the plan and aren't paid for under Original Medicare. Most Medicare Advantage Plans offer prescription drug coverage.

Medicare Advantage Prescription Drug (MA-PD) Plan

A Medicare Advantage plan that offers Medicare prescription drug coverage (Part D), Part A, and Part B benefits in one plan.

Medicare-Approved Amount (MAA)

In Original Medicare, this is the amount a doctor or supplier that accepts assignment can be paid. It may be less than the actual amount a doctor or supplier charges. Medicare pays part of this amount and you're responsible for the difference.

Medicare-approved supplier

A company, person, or agency that's been certified by Medicare to give you a medical item or service, except when you're an inpatient in a hospital or skilled nursing facility.

Medicare-certified provider

A health care provider (like a home health agency, hospital, nursing home, or dialysis facility) that's been approved by Medicare. Providers are approved or "certified" by Medicare if they've passed an inspection conducted by a state government agency. Medicare only covers care given by providers who are certified.

Medicare Cost Plan

A type of Medicare health plan available in some areas. In a Medicare Cost Plan, if you get services outside of the plan's network without a referral, your Medicare-covered services will be paid for under Original Medicare (your Cost Plan pays for emergency services or urgently needed services).

Medicare Health Maintenance Organization (HMO) Plan

A type of Medicare Advantage Plan (Part C) available in some areas of the country. In most

HMOs, you can only go to doctors, specialists, or hospitals on the plan's list except in an emergency. Most HMOs also require you to get a referral from your primary care physician.

Medicare health plan

Generally, a plan offered by a private company that contracts with Medicare to provide Part A and Part B benefits to people with Medicare who enroll in the plan. Medicare health plans include all Medicare Advantage Plans, Medicare Cost Plans, and Demonstration/Pilot Programs. Programs of All-inclusive Care for the Elderly (PACE) organizations are special types of Medicare health plans. PACE plans can be offered by public or private companies and provide Part D and other benefits in addition to Part A and Part B benefits.

Medicare Medical Savings Account (MSA) Plan

MSA Plans combine a high deductible Medicare Advantage Plan and a bank account. The plan deposits money from Medicare into the account. You can use the money in this account to pay for your health care costs, but only Medicare-covered expenses count toward your deductible. The amount deposited is usually less than your deductible amount so you generally will have to pay out-of-pocket before your coverage begins.

Medicare Part A (Hospital Insurance)

Part A covers inpatient hospital stays, care in a skilled nursing facility, hospice care, and some home health care.

Medicare Part B (Medical Insurance)

Part B covers certain doctors' services, outpatient care, medical supplies, and preventive services.

Medicare Part C

Also known as Medicare Advantage, this is a plan administered by a private insurer to administer and provide all of a participant's Part A and Part B benefits within a coordinated care system (HMO, PPO, etc.) See Medicare Advantage, above

Medicare plan

Any way other than Original Medicare that you can get your Medicare health or prescription drug coverage. This term includes all Medicare health plans and Medicare Prescription Drug Plans.

Medicare Preferred Provider Organization (PPO) Plan

A type of Medicare Advantage Plan (Part C) available in some areas of the country in which you pay less if you use doctors, hospitals, and other health care providers that belong to the plan's network. You can use doctors, hospitals, and providers outside of the network for an additional cost.

Medicare Prescription Drug Plan (Part D); PDP

Part D adds prescription drug coverage to Original Medicare, some Medicare Cost Plans, some Medicare Private-Fee-for-Service Plans, and Medicare Medical Savings Account Plans. These plans are offered by insurance companies and other private companies approved by Medicare. Many Medicare Advantage Plans may also offer prescription drug coverage that follows the same rules as Medicare Prescription Drug Plans.

Medicare Private Fee-for-Service (PFFS) Plan

A type of Medicare Advantage Plan (Part C) in which you can generally go to any doctor or hospital you could go to if you had Original Medicare, if the doctor or hospital agrees to treat you. The plan determines how much it will pay doctors and hospitals, and how much you must pay when you get care. A Private Fee-for-Service Plan is very different than Original Medicare, and you must follow the plan rules carefully when you go for health care services. When you're in a Private

Fee-for-Service Plan, you may pay more or less for Medicare-covered benefits than in Original Medicare.

Medicare Savings Program

A Medicaid program that helps people with limited income and resources pay some or all of their Medicare premiums, deductibles, and coinsurance.

Medicare SELECT

A type of Medigap policy that may cost a lower premium, but requires you to use hospitals and, in some cases, doctors within its network to be eligible for full benefits. Restricts Medigap plan members from using the all-inclusive system of all nationwide Medicare providers. Only available in certain areas, and becoming less popular.

Medicare Special Needs Plan (SNP)

A special type of Medicare Advantage Plan (Part C) that provides more focused and specialized health care for specific groups of people, like those who have both Medicare and Medicaid, who live in a nursing home, or have certain chronic medical conditions.

Medicare Summary Notice (MSN)

A notice you get after the doctor, other health care provider, or supplier files a claim for Part A or

Part B services in Original Medicare. It explains what the doctor, other health care provider, or supplier billed for, the Medicare-approved amount, how much Medicare paid, and what you must pay.

Medigap basic benefits

Benefits that all Medigap policies must cover, including Part A and Part B coinsurance amounts, blood, and additional hospital benefits not covered by Original Medicare.

Medigap Open Enrollment Period

A one-time only, 6-month period when federal law allows you to buy any Medigap policy you want that's sold in your state without any medical underwriting whatsoever. It starts in the first month that you're covered under Part B and you're age 65 or older. During this period, you can't be denied a Medigap policy or charged more due to past or present health problems. Some states may have additional open enrollment rights under state law.

Medigap policy

Medicare Supplement Insurance sold by private insurance companies to fill "gaps" in Original Medicare coverage. The gaps are potentially very large, and are created by deductibles, co-payments, and coinsurance required to be paid out of pocket by Medicare beneficiaries.

Multi-employer plan

In general, a group health plan that's sponsored jointly by 2 or more employers.

Network

The facilities, providers, and suppliers your health insurer or plan has contracted with to provide health care services.

Network pharmacies

Pharmacies that have agreed to provide members of certain Medicare plans with services and supplies at a discounted price. In some Medicare plans, your prescriptions are only covered if you get them filled at network pharmacies.

NONinsurance

Our suggested replacement for the word "coinsurance", since it means the portion of costs for which you have no insurance coverage in Original Medicare

Non-preferred pharmacy

A pharmacy that's part of a Medicare drug plan's network, but isn't a preferred pharmacy. You may pay higher out-of-pocket costs if you get your prescription drugs from a non-preferred pharmacy instead of a preferred pharmacy.

Occupational therapy

Treatment that helps you return to your usual activities (like bathing, preparing meals, and housekeeping) after an illness.

Open Election Period (OEP)

The re- introduction of Medicare Open Election Period in 2019 means a new enrollment period (actually and old one that is coming back) will be starting on January 1, 2019. This comes as as result of the 21st Century Cures Act.

The new enrollment period will run from January 1st through March 31st and will allow Medicare Advantage Plan members to dis-enroll from their current plan and switch to a different Medicare Advantage plan one time only. They can also dis-enroll from an advantage plan and go back to Original Medicare and then purchase a supplement and/or a PDP. Just like with the MA-PD, they can only enroll in the PDP plan if they had drug coverage with the MA-PD they dropped.

Optional supplemental benefits

Services that Medicare doesn't cover, but that a Medicare health plan may choose to offer. If you enroll in a plan with these services, you may choose to buy the services. If you choose to buy these benefits, you'll pay for them directly, usually as a premium, copayment, and/or coinsurance. These services may be offered individually or as a group of services, and they may be different for each Medicare health plan.

Original Medicare (OM)

Original Medicare is a fee-for-service health plan that has two parts: Part A (Hospital Insurance) and Part B (Medical Insurance). After you pay a deductible, Medicare pays its share of the Medicare-approved amount, and you pay your share (coinsurance and co-pays).

Out-of-network

A benefit that may be provided by your Medicare Advantage plan. Generally, this benefit gives you the choice to get plan services from outside of the plan's network of health care providers. In some cases, your out-of-pocket costs may be higher for an out-of-network benefit.

Out-of-pocket costs

Health or prescription drug costs that you must pay on your own because they aren't covered by Medicare or other insurance. The technical Part D definition of True Out of Pocket Costs (TrOOP) includes the discount "paid" by Brand name drug manufacturers/

Outpatient hospital care

Medical or surgical care you get from a

hospital when your doctor hasn't written an order to admit you to the hospital as an inpatient. Outpatient hospital care may include emergency department services, observation services, outpatient surgery, lab tests, or X-rays. Your care may be considered outpatient hospital care even if you spend the night at the hospital.

This can result in not qualifying for Medicare benefits with a subsequent nursing home stay, or the non-payment of hospital bills as a Part A benefit.

Hospitals and doctors often use this as a (shady) tool to avoid CMS penalties for excessive readmissions following a prior inpatient stay. It can result in large additional out of pocket costs for the patient.

PACE

See Programs for All-inclusive Care for the Elderly, below

Pap test

A test to check for cancer of the cervix, the opening to a woman's uterus. It's done by removing cells from the cervix. The cells are then prepared so they can be seen under a microscope.

Part A, B, C, D

See Medicare Part A, etc., above

Patient lifts

A medical device used to lift you from a bed or wheelchair.

Pelvic exam

An exam to check if internal female organs are normal by feeling their shape and size.

Penalty

An amount added to your monthly premium for Part A, Part B or a Medicare drug plan (Part D) if you don't join when you're first eligible. You pay this higher amount as long as you have Medicare. There are some exceptions for circumstances considered by CMS to be valid reasons for missing deadlines.

Pharmacy network

Pharmacies that have agreed to provide members of certain Medicare plans with services and supplies at a discounted price. In some Medicare plans, your prescriptions are only covered if you get them filled at network pharmacies.

Physical therapy

Treatment of an injury or a disease by mechanical means, like exercise, massage, heat, and light treatment.

Podiatrist

Foot doctor. Foot care is specifically excluded from standard Part B benefits in most cases.

Point-of-service option

In a Health Maintenance Organization (HMO), this option lets you use doctors and hospitals outside the plan for an additional cost.

Power of attorney

A medical power of attorney is a document that lets you appoint someone you trust to make decisions about your medical care. This type of advance directive also may be called a health care proxy, appointment of health care agent, or a durable power of attorney for health care.

Pre-existing condition

A health problem you had before the date that new health coverage starts. Medigap insurance in most cases uses a "6 and 6 rule", meaning that a condition treated or recognized within the past 6 months can only be excluded from coverage for the next 6 months.

Preferred pharmacy

A pharmacy that's part of a Medicare drug plan's network. You pay lower out-of-pocket costs if you get your prescription drugs from a preferred pharmacy instead of a non-preferred pharmacy.

Premium

The periodic payment to Medicare, an insurance company, or a health care plan for health or prescription drug coverage.

Preventive services

ss at an early stage, when treatment is likely to work best (for example, preventive services include Pap tests, flu shots, and screening mammograms).

Primary Care Physician (PCP)

The doctor you see first for most health problems. He or she makes sure you get the care you need to keep you healthy. He or she also may talk with other doctors and health care providers about your care and refer you to them. In many Medicare Advantage Plans, you must see your primary care doctor before you see any other health care provider.

Prior authorization

Approval that you must get from a Medicare drug plan before you fill your prescription in order for the prescription to be covered by your plan. Your Medicare drug plan may require prior authorization for certain drugs.

Private add-ons

Insurance plans sold and administered by licensed private insurance companies, designed to interface with the public insurance scheme of Medicare. There are three main types: Medicare

Advantage (a/k/a Part C plans); Prescription Drug Plans (a/k/a Part D plans, PDP); and Medicare Supplement plans (a/k/a Medigap plans).

Programs of All-inclusive Care for the Elderly (PACE)

A special type of health plan that provides all the care and services covered by Medicare and Medicaid as well as additional medically necessary care and services based on your needs as determined by an interdisciplinary team. PACE serves frail older adults who need nursing home services but are capable of living in the community. PACE combines medical, social, and long-term care services and prescription drug coverage.

Protective sensations

Feeling in the foot or leg that helps warn you that the skin is being injured. Nerve damage caused by diabetes can cause loss of feeling in the foot or leg, also known as "loss of protective sensations (LOPS)." This may result in skin loss, blisters, or ulcers.

QIC

Qualified Independent Contractor, an independent entity with which Medicare contracts to handle the reconsideration level of an Original Medicare (Part A or Part B) appeal.

QIO

Quality Improvement Organization, an organization of doctors and other health care experts under contract with Medicare that uses doctors and other health care experts to review complaints and quality of care for people with Medicare.

Qualified Disabled and Working Individuals (QDWI) Program

A state program that helps pay Part A premiums for people who have Part A and limited income and resources.

Qualified Individual (QI) Program

A state program that helps pay Part B premiums for people who have Part A and limited income and resources.

Qualified Medicare Beneficiary (QMB) Program

A state program that helps pay Part A premiums, Part B premiums, and other cost-sharing (like deductibles, coinsurance, and copayments) for people who have Part A and limited income and resources.

Referral

A written order from your primary care

doctor for you to see a specialist or get certain medical services. In many Health Maintenance Organizations (HMOs), you need to get a referral before you can get medical care from anyone except your primary care doctor. If you don't get a referral first, the plan may not pay for the services.

Rehabilitation services

Health care services that help you keep, get back, or improve skills and functioning for daily living that you've lost or have been impaired because you were sick, hurt, or disabled. These services may include physical and occupational therapy, speech-language pathology, and psychiatric rehabilitation services in a variety of inpatient and/or outpatient settings.

Religious nonmedical health care institution

A facility that provides nonmedical health care items and services to people who need hospital or skilled nursing facility care, but for whom that care would be inconsistent with their religious beliefs.

Respite care

Temporary care provided in a nursing home, hospice inpatient facility, or hospital so that a family member or friend who is the patient's caregiver can rest or take some time off.

Rider

An extra provision in an insurance contract which confers additional benefits, usually at additional premium cost.

Rural health clinic

A federally qualified health center (FQHC) that provides health care services in rural areas where there's a shortage of health care services.

Screening mammogram

A medical procedure to check for breast cancer before you or a doctor may be able to find it manually.

Secondary payer

The insurance policy, plan, or program that pays second on a claim for medical care. This could be Medicare, Medicaid, or other insurance depending on the situation.

Service area

A geographic area where a health insurance plan accepts members if it limits membership based on where people live. For plans that limit which doctors and hospitals you may use, it's also generally the area where you can get routine (non-emergency) services. The plan may disenroll you if you move out of the plan's service area.

Skilled nursing care

Care like intravenous injections that can only be given by a registered nurse or doctor.

Skilled nursing facility (SNF)

A nursing facility with the staff and equipment to give skilled nursing care and, in most cases, skilled rehabilitative services and other related health services.

Skilled nursing facility care

Skilled nursing care and rehabilitation services provided on a daily basis, in a skilled nursing facility (SNF). Examples of SNF care include physical therapy or intravenous injections that can only be given by a registered nurse or doctor.

Specified Low-Income Medicare Beneficiary (SLMB) Program

A state program that helps pay Part B premiums for people who have Part A and limited income and resources.

Speech-language therapy (speech-language pathology services)

Treatment that helps you strengthen or regain speech, language, and swallowing skills.

Star Rating (1-Star to 5-Star)

CMS produced rating system of Medicare Advantage plans, judged by internal metrics and satisfaction statistics of plan members.

State Health Insurance Assistance Program (SHIP)

A state program that gets money from the federal government to give free local health insurance counseling to people with Medicare, staffed largely by volunteers.

State Insurance Department

A state agency that regulates insurance and can provide information about Medigap policies and other private health insurance.

State Medical Assistance (Medicaid) office

A state or local agency that can give information about, and help with applications for, Medicaid programs that help pay medical bills for people with limited income and resources.

State Pharmaceutical Assistance Program (SPAP)

A state program that provides help paying for drug coverage based on financial need, age, or medical condition.

State Survey Agency

A state agency that oversees health care facilities that participate in the Medicare and/or Medicaid programs by, for example, inspecting health care facilities and investigating complaints to ensure that health and safety standards are met.

Step therapy

A coverage rule used by some Medicare Prescription Drug Plans that requires you to try one or more similar, lower cost drugs to treat your condition before the plan will cover the prescribed drug.

Subluxation

When one or more of the bones of your spine move out of position.

Supplemental Security Income (SSI)

A monthly benefit paid by Social Security to people with limited income and resources who are disabled, blind, or age 65 or older. SSI benefits aren't the same as Social Security retirement or disability benefits.

Supplier

Generally, any company, person, or agency that gives you a medical item or service, except when you're an inpatient in a hospital or skilled nursing facility.

Telemedicine

Medical or other health services given to a patient using a communications system (like a computer, phone, or television) by a practitioner in a location different than the patient's.

Tiers

Groups of drugs that have a different cost for each group. Generally, a drug in a lower tier will cost you less than a drug in a higher tier.

TRICARE

A health care program for active-duty and retired uniformed services members and their families.

TRICARE FOR LIFE (TFL)

Expanded medical coverage available to Medicare-eligible uniformed services retirees age 65 or older, their eligible family members and survivors, and certain former spouses.

TTY

A TTY (teletypewriter) is a communication device used by people who are deaf, hard-of-hearing, or have severe speech impairment. People who don't have a TTY can communicate with a TTY user through a message relay center (MRC). An MRC has TTY operators available to send and interpret TTY messages.

Urgently needed care

Care that you get outside of your Medicare health plan's service area for a sudden illness or injury that needs medical care right away but isn't life threatening. If it's not safe to wait until you get home to get care from a plan doctor, the health plan must pay for the care.

Workers' compensation

An insurance plan that employers are required to have to cover employees who get sick or injured on the job.

About the Authors

Bob Arndt is a former university Professor of Economics, a Tax Expert licensed by The Department of Treasury as an Enrolled Agent who recently turned 65 and began navigating the "Medicare Maze". It was a nightmare so he decided to dedicate himself to helping, coaching, advising and guiding fellow Seniors on the best, most timely decisions for their healthcare for the rest of their life. Because Medicare is the single most important aspect of retirement and financial planning for Seniors.

Bob has over 36 years of financial management and operating experience as both an Owner and Operator (President and Chief Financial Officer). Bob understands insurance and business because he has owned and operated companies in a variety of industries including cable television, internet services, main frame software services, restaurants and real estate.

He has been married for 45 years, has 3 children and nine grandchildren. He is a Fitness Practitioner and has won over 100 awards in various Sports/Contests. He has served on 15

Boards of Directors, graduated with honors from both Eastern Michigan University with a Master's Degree in Finance and Western Michigan University with a Bachelor of Business Administration. He can be reached at:

bob@GuardianTaxPro.com

Phone: (734) 444-5149

Rick Mortimer is an aging Baby Boomer living in the beautiful foothills of the North Carolina Piedmont. When he hit the 65-year mark, he began his personal journey through the maze of everything Medicare. He was dismayed by the complexity of the decisions that had to be made, the lack of available strategies for answering them, and the convolutions of the system in place to provide this vital set of services to over 57 million Americans.

Having first been licensed to sell health insurance in 1988, and working as a trust advisor for many years, he knew his way around the industry and the terminology very well. Even with this background, he found the process so daunting and confusing that he decided to come out of years of medically induced retirement and get re-licensed, so that he could help others facing the wall of questions that Medicare generates. After a career noted for serial entrepreneurship, this move quickly led to the founding of **Next Mountain Advisors Inc.**, a firm established to help fellow seniors navigate the changing requirements of living with an aging body, and a fixed or declining set of resources.

Mortimer has also seen the inside of the healthcare system as a too-often patient, surviving the challenges of prostate cancer and proton beam therapy, congestive heart failure and A-fib, near death after a stenting procedure, multiple ablations and other heart procedures, a deep staph infection caused by knee surgery, and now a diagnosis of Parkinsons disease. His new mission is what keeps him alive, and focused on delivering as much value to others as possible in his remaining years.

He is also the founder of the new American Association of Professional Medicare Agents, at **MedicarePros.org,** an organization dedicated to supporting and codifying the practice of impartially and thoroughly educating seniors on the decisions they face, and helping them get the products and services they need.

He works personally with clients all over North Carolina, and is available to speak at senior-focused events anywhere. He can be reached at

rick@NextMountainAdvisors.com

Toll free: (866) 468-9086

Made in the USA
Monee, IL
04 November 2026

67386585R00154